THE DEVELOPERS' GUIDE TO PLANNING AND DESIGNING LOGISTICS CENTERS IN CAREC COUNTRIES

APRIL 2023

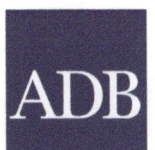

CONTENTS

TABLES, FIGURES, AND BOXES

PREFACE

Research for *The Developers' Guide to Planning and Designing Logistics Centers in CAREC Countries* began in March 2022. The author conducted one field trip to Georgia, Kazakhstan, and Uzbekistan in June, visiting a variety of projects and meeting relevant stakeholders. Consultations were also carried out online with stakeholders in Azerbaijan during June–July. The resulting guide was circulated for review among development partners and Central Asia Regional Economic Cooperation (CAREC) member countries in July and August, and feedback was received up to September. It was then presented at the CAREC Transport Sector Coordination Committee Meeting held in Almaty in October 2022. The author is Ignasi Ragas Prat, logistics facilities consultant.

ABBREVIATIONS

CAREC	Central Asia Regional Economic Cooperation
CIS	Commonwealth of Independent States
GDP	gross domestic product
ha	hectare
ICD	inland container depot
IT	information technology
LC	logistics center
m	meter
m^2	square meter
PPP	public–private partnership
PRC	People's Republic of China
SEZ	special economic zone
t	metric ton
TLC	transport and logistics center

EXECUTIVE SUMMARY

Logistics centers (LCs) as defined in this guide are complexes that have been specifically conceived and designed to accommodate warehouses, other transport and logistics facilities, and associated services. LCs exist in a variety of names across the world. LCs create environments where transport and logistics activities can be performed more efficiently than when these are not clustered together thus reducing their environmental and land consumption footprint.

Many countries in recent decades have seen LCs successfully developed for a variety of purposes, including relocating obsolete transport and distribution facilities from their inner cities, attracting additional business to ports and airports, encouraging intermodal transport, organizing land use in the surrounds of cities, and promoting the development and modernization of transport and logistics businesses. While some Central Asia Regional Economic Cooperation (CAREC) countries are already experiencing the development of LCs, the concept is still a novelty in others.

The design and layout of LCs involve some specificities that are not always required in conventional industrial parks, and this may translate to more complex and costlier development. A wide range of business models have been used to develop LCs around the world. Since LCs are regarded as tools to achieve some economic, social, or environmental objectives, they may benefit from some public sector involvement. However, governments need to fully understand how location, layout, and business model underpin the success of an LC.

Growth in consumption, transport, and trade opportunities stemming from the geographic positions of CAREC countries as well as new logistics trends are triggering interest in LCs. Location and conditions of some legacy logistics infrastructure in CAREC countries are incompatible with modern logistics practice hence the development of new facilities is urgent. On the positive side, many CAREC countries benefit from competitive rail freight, relatively low land availability constraints, and familiarity with international logistics practices.

The Developers' Guide to Planning and Designing Logistics Centers in CAREC Countries aims to

(i)   bring clarity to the concept and policies supporting LCs (Section 2);
(ii) provide guidance on the design and layout of LCs (Section 3);
(iii) describe the steps to successful implementation and operation of LCs (Section 4);
(iv) inform about LCs' economic, social, and environmental impacts (Section 5); and
(v)   identify trends, opportunities, and challenges for the CAREC region (Section 6).

The target audiences of this guide are public and private sector stakeholders in the CAREC region.

1

INTRODUCTION

1.1 Why This Guide?

Many countries have included the development of logistics centers (LCs) in their transport policies and programs in recent decades via a variety of institutional arrangements and business models. However, some projects envisaged in programs and plans have failed to materialize, failed to attract forecasted demand, or have not achieved the targets set at their launch for various reasons, such as the location or business model proving to be inappropriate, or failing to align with private sector demand or operational needs.

Governments and stakeholders in developing countries may benefit from taking stock from these experiences when they include LCs in their transport sector policies and plans. However, drawing lessons from experiences in other regions may be a challenge for non-familiarized decision makers and technical staff for several reasons, starting with a confusion created by many labels used to describe LCs, such as freight villages, freight cities, interports, distriparks, inland ports, logistics hubs, logistics parks, and distribution hubs.

The Developers' Guide to Planning and Designing Logistics Centers in CAREC Countries has been prepared to bring clarity to concepts and provide guidance on market, institutional, planning, financial, and operational issues relevant to the concept, design, implementation, and governance of LCs.

Through the Central Asia Regional Economic Cooperation (CAREC) program, work has concentrated on transport and trade facilitation. Recent CAREC research in the field of logistics has highlighted the significance of shortcomings in other fields, one of them being the quality and standards of logistics infrastructure.[1] This guide also aims to fill knowledge gaps, so that planning and delivery of logistics projects in CAREC countries can be enhanced.

1.2 What Are the Specificities of CAREC Countries Regarding Logistics Centers Development?

LCs are already operational in the region, including in Kazakhstan and to a lesser extent in Uzbekistan, Azerbaijan, and Pakistan. Interest in more LCs is high, as evident from the number of projects that have been presented at CAREC meetings in recent years and have appeared in government statements and the media. A non-exhaustive list of projects is outlined in Appendix 1.

The CAREC region encompasses very different countries, making a one-size-fits-all approach impossible. However, some specificities are relevant for LC development. They include:

• Some CAREC countries have significant internal markets, such as Pakistan with a population of 221 million, and Uzbekistan with 34 million people.

---

[1]   Asian Development Bank (ADB). 2021. *Ports and Logistics Scoping Study in CAREC Countries.* Manila. https://www.adb.org/publications/ports-logistics-scoping-study-carec-countries.

Kazakhstan has a much lower population of 19 million, but a higher purchasing power, with gross domestic product (GDP) per capita of $9,000, compared with $1,200 for Pakistan and $1,700 for Uzbekistan. Other countries such as Georgia (with a population of 4 million and GDP per capita of $4,200), the Kyrgyz Republic (7 million people, $1,200 GDP per capita), and Tajikistan (10 million people, GDP per capita of $860) have rather small markets.[2] Since the size and sophistication of a logistics business is correlated with its volumes and the value of its cargo, the adoption of modern concepts in logistics infrastructure and practice is more challenging in some countries than in others.

- In most CAREC countries, labor costs are relatively low so that logistics operators have little incentive to modernize facilities and procedures and invest in automation.
- In some countries, notably those of the former Soviet Union, there is ample availability of obsolete but cheap facilities built during Soviet times. Many operators see little reason to relocate operations to more modern facilities, and may struggle to cope with the capital expenditure costs required to build new facilities.

- Railways still play a pivotal role in transport and logistics chains in many countries, both for containerized cargo and for breakbulk. This influences the location patterns and layouts of many logistics facilities, but also results in legacy and sometimes underperforming facilities. Most rail cargo terminals are still located in legacy inner-city locations, benefiting from the fact that there is still little competition for rail capacity from commuter and other passenger trains.
- Government policies have focused on developing transport corridors and linear infrastructure, i.e., building/upgrading road and rail networks, but less attention has been given to nodal transport infrastructure, i.e., terminals and LCs.
- City logistics policies at the local/municipal level are at very early stages. Some inner-city terminals and logistics facilities already encroached by urban areas face inefficiencies in logistics operations, external costs from heavy cargo moving on city roads, opportunity costs of keeping land-intensive activities in downtown areas, industrial and road safety hazards, and other challenges.

Soviet-era buildings now used as warehouses. A warehouse in Tbilisi, Georgia (left), and one in Astana, Kazakhstan (right) (photos by author).

2   World Bank. World Bank Data. https://data.worldbank.org/country (accessed May 2022). Figures are rounded.

2 CONCEPTS AND RATIONALE

2.1 The Importance of Logistics to the Economy

2.1.1 What is logistics?

According to the Council of Supply Chain Management, logistics is that part of supply chain management that plans, implements, and controls the efficient and effective forward and reverse flow and storage of goods, services, and related information between the point of origin and the point of consumption to meet customers' requirements.[3]

2.1.2 Why should policy makers care about logistics?

Policy makers should care about logistics because:

- Logistics delivers items needed by people. This was most evident during coronavirus disease lockdowns. Better logistics increases product availability and lowers prices for consumers.
- Logistics creates direct and indirect employment. It is evolving from an in-house activity to a specialized industry, offering a wide range of job opportunities.
- Lower logistics costs lead to more competitive companies.

- Efficient and resilient supply chains increase the robustness and modernization of the economy. Integration into modern supply chains is conducive to updated manufacturing and distribution practices compliant with international standards.
- Logistics influences people's quality of life. Underperforming and disorganized logistics systems aggravate traffic congestion, noise, pollution, accidents, and lead to overconsumption of land and natural resources. Well-organized location patterns for logistics activities reduce these impacts.
- Transport and logistics influence the achievement of high-level environmental and climate change objectives.[4]

2.1.3 What policy levers can be used to improve logistics performance?

Governments can improve logistics performance through

- investing in transport infrastructure to reduce transit time and costs, and increase safety;
- training and capability schemes to improve the productivity and value added of the workforce in logistics;

---

[3] Council of Supply Chain Management Professionals. 2022. *CSCMP Supply Chain Management Definitions and Glossary.* https://cscmp.org/CSCMP/Educate/SCM_Definitions_and_Glossary_of_Terms.aspx.

[4] United Nations Economic Commission for Europe (UNECE). 2021. *Handbook for National Master Plans for Freight Transport and Logistics.* Geneva. https://unece.org/transport/publications/handbook-national-master-plans-freight-transport-and-logistics.

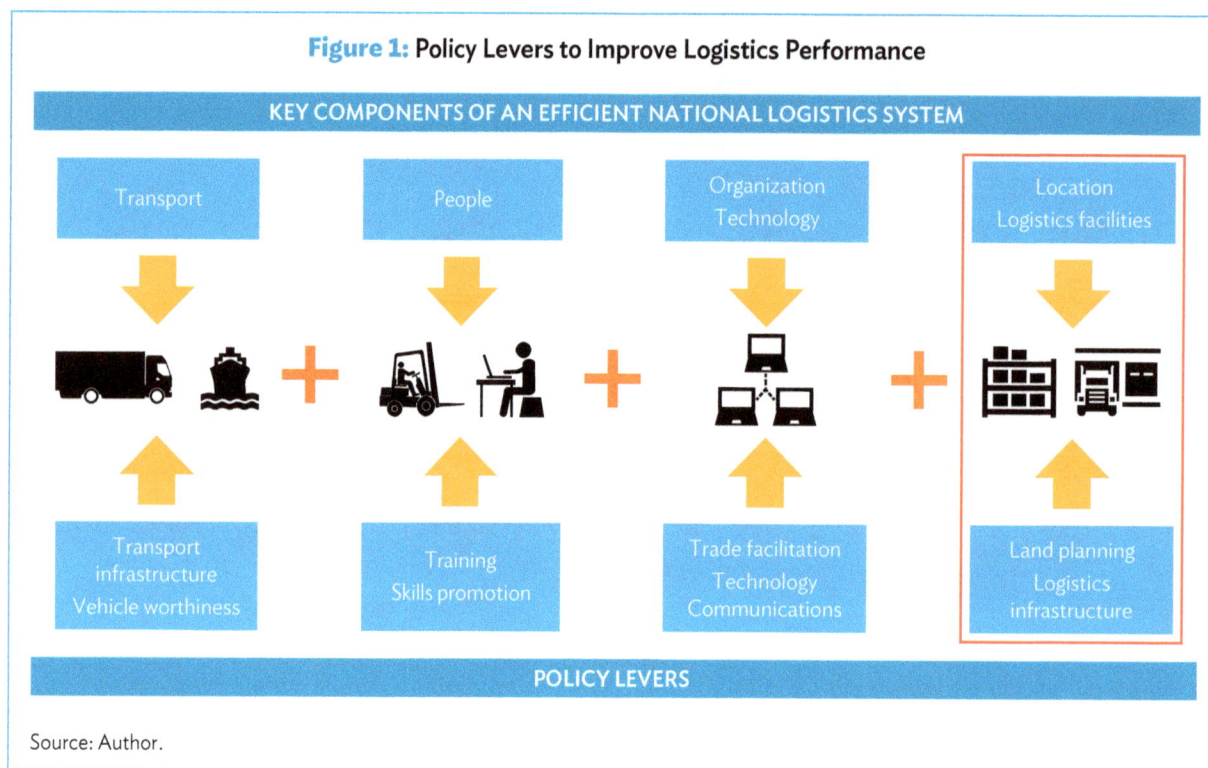

Figure 1: Policy Levers to Improve Logistics Performance

Source: Author.

- trade facilitation, process reengineering, and communications and information technology (IT) to streamline procedures to avoid wasting time and resources; and
- planning, regulation, and investment to facilitate logistics activities being performed in efficient facilities in the best possible locations.

Among the levers illustrated in Figure 1, this guide focuses on the fourth.

2.2 Logistics Centers' Concept and Purpose

2.2.1 What is a logistics center?

Warehouses may cluster spontaneously in a specific area or around transport infrastructure. In this guide we define an LC as a complex specifically conceived and designed to accommodate warehouses, transport and logistics facilities, and other associated services.

Specific location, layout, and associated services, both to improve operational performance and create synergies among companies, are the main value propositions of LCs as compared with conventional industrial parks.

There is no universally accepted definition of an LC. Box 1 shows some examples of definitions at the international and national levels.

2.2.2 What are the advantages of logistics centers?

In most countries, any private entrepreneur can build a warehouse on a plot of land where land use regulations allow such industrial activities. In some places where land use and zoning regulations are nonexistent or their enforcement is weak, warehouses may be built on farmland because it is cheaper that in industrial estates. This may lead to atomized and anarchic location patterns of logistics platforms, without proper access roads, leading to intense movement of trucks

Box 1: International and National Definitions of Logistics Centers

United Nations Economic and Social Commission for Europe

The United Nations Economic and Social Commission for Europe (UNECE) defines a logistics center (LC) as a:

> ...geographical grouping of independent companies and bodies which are dealing with freight transport (for example, freight forwarders, shippers, transport operators, customs) and with accompanying services (for example, storage, maintenance and repair), including at least a terminal.[a]

Europlatforms

Europlatforms is a federation of LC developers and operators in Europe. Its definition of an LC is more developed than UNECE's and does not require the inclusion of a rail terminal:

> A Logistics Center is a center in a defined area within which all activities relating to transport, logistics and the distribution of goods—both for national and international transit, are carried out by various operators on a commercial basis. The operators can either be owners or tenants of buildings and facilities (warehouses, distribution centers, storage areas, offices, truck services, etc.), which have been built here.

> In order to comply with free competition rules, a Logistics Center must be open to allow access to any company involved in the activities set out above. A Logistics Center must also be equipped with all facilities to carry out the mentioned operations. If possible, it should include public services for the staff and equipment for the users.

> In order to encourage intermodal transport for the handling of goods, a Logistics Center should preferably be served by a multiplicity of transport modes (road, rail, sea, inland waterway, air). To ensure synergy and commercial cooperation, it is important that a Logistics Center is managed in a single and neutral legal body (preferably by a Public–Private Partnership). Finally, a Logistics Center must comply with European standards and quality performance to provide the framework for commercial and sustainable transport solutions.[b]

Kazakhstan

Kazakhstan's Law on Transport defines transport and logistics centers (TLC) as:

> ...transport infrastructure that includes a specially designated area with facilities designed to perform preparatory, distribution and final technological operations for cargo and vehicles involved in their transport, including inspection, customs and border operations in accordance with the legislation of the Republic of Kazakhstan (art 1, 5-1).[c]

A TLC may be international, i.e., designed to perform operations across the customs border of the Eurasian Economic Union (comprising Armenia, Belarus, Kazakhstan, the Kyrgyz Republic, and the Russian Federation) thus including inspection, customs and border operations, or regional, i.e., designed to carry out operations within the economic union.

A 2015 Executive Order of the Ministry for Investment and Development[d] meanwhile sets some standard requirements for organization facilities at a TLC, including:

- The TLC must be located near highways, airports, sea or river ports, or railway stations.
- Access roads must ensure efficient movements and internal roads must provide unhindered maneuvering and access to loading and unloading points, with a recommended road width of 3.5 to 4.5 meters.
- Administrative buildings must have rooms for accommodating server and communication nodes.
- The TLC must be a fenced and alarm-secured area with controlled access and a video-surveillance system that can monitor the vehicle parking area.

continued on next page

Box 1: continued

- Certified weighing equipment must correspond to the nature of the placed goods and vehicles.
- The TLC must have backup power supply systems.
- International TLCs must include spaces for customs and inspections as well as office space for necessary government bodies. Service facilities such as food points, bank terminals, currency exchange points, and post office are also needed.

[a] UNECE. 2001. *Terminology on Combined Transport*. New York and Geneva. https://unece.org/DAM/trans/wp24/documents/term.pdf.
[b] EUROPLATFORMS EEIG. The European Logistic Platforms Association. *Definition of Logistics Center*. Brussels. http://europlatforms.eu/Logistic%20CenterDefinition.html.
[c] The Law of Kazakhstan "On Transport" dated 21 September 1994 and amended in 1998 and 2004.
[d] Executive Order of the Ministry for Investment and Development dated 28 May 2015, No. 650. "On Approval of Standard Requirements for Arrangement and Technical Equipment of Transport and Logistics Centers."

through places not prepared for them, creating unexpected nuisances to neighboring residents and businesses, and making transport and logistics companies operate from inappropriate locations and at underperforming facilities.

In contrast, clustering logistics platforms in defined areas, i.e., in logistics centers, with good access to transport infrastructure, may bring the following benefits:[5]

- Improved productivity for logistics and transport companies through better connectivity and reduced transport costs. Productivity is further improved when an LC's layout is specifically designed to optimize logistics operations (Section 3.2).
- Improved modernization, as they create opportunities to share knowledge and the incentive to emulate the best performer. Thus, LCs create an environment conducive to the transformation of transport companies into value-added logistics operators (Figure 9).

- New opportunities for inter-company cooperation and synergies by creating a basis for sharing resources, collaborative projects, pooling of services, and lobbying government with a single voice.
- As LCs are often controlled, video-surveyed precincts, they can reduce pilferage and insurance costs.

2.2.3 Why should governments be interested in logistics centers?

Governments in many parts of the world have been active in planning and developing LCs for a variety of reasons. These include:

- Reducing land consumption and environmental impacts of logistics through the allocation of land earmarked to logistics activities in locations where these impacts are minimized;

---

[5]   To learn more about these and other benefits see: Y. Sheffi. 2013. Logistics-Intensive Clusters: Global Competitiveness and Regional Growth. In J. H. Bookbinder ed. *Handbook of Global Logistics* (pp. 463–500). New York; V. D. Heuvel et al. 2012. Co-Location Synergies: Specialized Versus Diverse Logistics. *BETA publicatie: Working Papers* Vol. 388; I. Ragas and F. Manchon. 2017. *Design and Implementation of Logistics Platforms*. LOGISMED Regional Initiative – CETMO. Barcelona.

Logistics performed at unsuitable locations. Clockwise from above left: Unsuitable access roads to logistics facilities cause congestion and risks in Cundinamarca, Colombia; misappropriation of urban space by logistics equipment in Casablanca, Morocco; suboptimal warehouses and unpaved yard in Montevideo, Uruguay; and an encroached warehouse in a dense urban area of Karachi, Pakistan (photos by author, except below right, by Adrian Sammons).

- Promoting intermodality and multimodality through clustering logistics activities adjacent to intermodal infrastructure;
- Modernizing transport and logistics sectors, as LCs provide critical mass for capacity building and training activities, investment in IT, etc.;
- Stimulating the upgrading of logistics buildings standards in terms of quality of construction, operations, environment, and safety;
- Facilitating frameworks for public–private cooperation that may enable the structuration of logistics clusters and their promotion at national and international levels;
- Creating economies of scale for the provision of government functions, e.g., customs and inspections, vehicle worthiness tests, and driver training facilities;

- Promoting jobs and attracting business, as logistics can catalyze jobs in other related sectors; and
- Promoting companies' involvement in the maintenance of shared space and facilities. Companies in LCs have similar activities and needs, which makes it easier that they agree on pooling resources to fund security services, maintenance, waste management, and so on, thus leading to higher levels of upkeep and tidiness than in standard industrial areas.

2.2.4 Do logistics centers have drawbacks?

Yes, drawbacks exist, and it is useful to identify them to prepare mitigation if required. Table 1 provides several explanations.

Table 1: Drawbacks of Logistics Centers for Companies and Hosts

Drawbacks for Companies	Drawbacks for Hosts
• Concentration of companies make them more vulnerable to disruptions due to industrial action or union strikes. LC managers should have open communication with industrial unions to agree on minimum operational conditions.	• Increased wear and tear of transport infrastructure due to intensive use by heavy trucks. Budgets to infrastructure maintenance need to be increased.
• Some companies may feel uncomfortable located beside their competitors. LC managers should be transparent and impartial in the face of all companies located in the LC.	• Risk of opposition from residents. Developers should be active in engaging residents in the planning and development stages of an LC, including regarding compensation and local hiring policies.
• Proximity facilitates talent hunt among companies. Mitigation is complex but the LC management could encourage a good practice agreement among companies.	• Risk of excess reliance on a single economic sector. Communities should engage in economic diversification policies.

LC = logistics center.
Source: Author.

2.2.5 What policies can governments use to promote LCs?

Policies to promote LCs are subject to governments' willingness and resources, and can take the following approaches (ordered according to public sector involvement, from low to high):

- The simpler approach is setting broad policy goals and encouraging actors, either in the public sector (e.g., port authorities, railways entities, and development agencies), or private sector to follow the direction, sometimes facilitated by incentives.
- A further step is to formulate a scheme where locations for LCs, implementing procedures, and financial resources are proposed. Quite often these schemes are set at strategic level before feasibility analysis of projects, or the detailed definition of sites has been set. Despite their limits, these schemes may be useful to mobilize interested parties, align strategies, and prepare the ground for further steps. On the downside, pointing at locations without quick intervention may lead to sharp increases in land prices and compromise the feasibility of the project before its start.
- Another step is made when specific locations are defined, and land use regulations clearly state their logistics vocation. Logistics projects can materialize in the short or long term.

What is mostly relevant is that zoning regulations protect a strategic site (e.g., one close to an existing or planned port, major road, or other infrastructure) from alternative land uses that could be incompatible with future logistics developments. This step may require some level of inter-institutional cooperation since land-use and zoning regulations are often within the jurisdiction of municipal or local governments (see Section 4.1.2).

- A government may be willing to invest money in LC projects. This can take the form of funding project preparations (e.g., feasibility studies and engineering studies), or even funding land acquisition and resettlement. Often project sites set by LC schemes are already on government-controlled land to avoid speculative movements and price hikes. Occasionally, governments fund off-site infrastructure, such as access roads, rail infrastructure, and drainage works.
- Government interventions mentioned so far do not necessarily predetermine the nature of the developer. A qualitative leap happens when a government decides to be directly involved in the development of an LC and creates a vehicle (e.g., a government undertaking or a state-owned enterprise). This vehicle can operate on its own or engage in a joint venture with private sector partners. A variety of forms and their implications are discussed in Section 4.2.2.

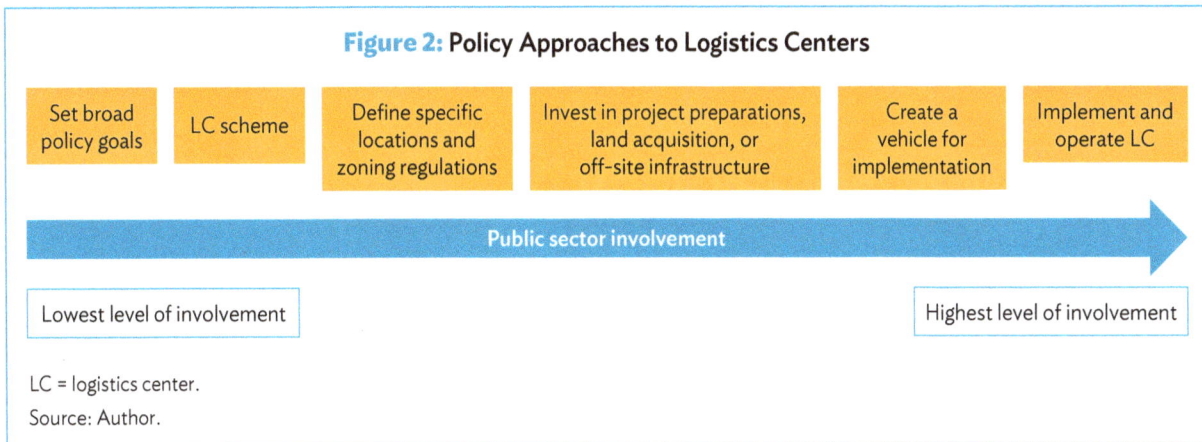

Figure 2: Policy Approaches to Logistics Centers

| Set broad policy goals | LC scheme | Define specific locations and zoning regulations | Invest in project preparations, land acquisition, or off-site infrastructure | Create a vehicle for implementation | Implement and operate LC |

Public sector involvement

| Lowest level of involvement | | Highest level of involvement |

LC = logistics center.
Source: Author.

- The involvement of the public sector vehicle may stop once construction works are finished, or continue in the form of an LC manager. See Sections 4.3.1 and 4.3.2.

Policy approaches are summarized in Figure 2.

It is worth highlighting that LC policies can be set and implemented both at national government level and at subnational government level. In fact, some of the most successful policies in Europe and the United States have been implemented by subnational government entities.

2.2.6 Where and why was the concept of logistics centers started?

LCs were not "invented" in any specific place, nor do they have any defined paternity. The conceptualization of nodes clustering transport and logistics activities was achieved organically through experiences in different countries. Some were born as port initiatives, others were closely linked to road transport, urban redevelopment schemes, or the relocation of wholesale food markets.

Stemming from these origins, a wide range of names, acronyms, and labels have been created in different parts of the world to denominate rather similar concepts.

This variety of names has sometimes obscured the concept of LCs to laypeople. Broadly speaking, most names refer to the same LC concept defined in this guide. We use the term "logistics center" because it is neutral and not associated with any specific brand or developer.

Appendix 2 includes some examples of LCs developed in Europe and the United States, illustrating a variety of sizes, purposes, type of developers, business models, and outcomes.

2.2.7 What are the differences between a special economic zone and a logistics center?

Free zones, free economic zones, or special economic zones (SEZs) are defined areas exempted from import and export duties, and also potentially benefiting from specific tax, corporate, labor, rules of origin, and other regulations as a means to attract inward investment.

In essence, free economic zones or SEZs are different from conventional business or industrial parks due to their specific regulatory environment, and what makes LCs different is their physical location, infrastructure, and layout. These may overlap, i.e., an SEZ adjacent to a major infrastructure hub featuring a logistics-centered layout and infrastructure. However, typically SEZs target a wider range of activities, such as manufacturing and services, that extend beyond the typical targets of LCs.

3

TECHNICAL FEATURES OF LOGISTICS CENTERS

3.1 Warehouses, Functions, and Locations

3.1.1 What are the functions of a warehouse and what is its place in a supply chain?

Warehouses may cover a variety of activities depending on their function in the supply chain. These functions influence their size, layout, and location. The possible functions of warehouses, usually termed "platforms" in logistics jargon, are illustrated in Figure 3.[6]

Gateway platforms

Gateway platforms are located adjacent or close to breakpoints in transport chains. These breakpoints may be port terminals where cargo is transshipped from vessels to land transport vehicles (trucks or trains) or air cargo terminals where cargo is moved from airplanes to trucks.[7] Breakpoints may also be related to transshipments of rail to rail or truck to truck for technical, operational, or regulatory reasons.

As an example, the rail gauge in the People's Republic of China (PRC), Türkiye, and Iran is different to that in Commonwealth of Independent States (CIS) countries, making rail to rail transshipment imperative.[8] This technical breakpoint has promoted the emergence of logistics facilities in places such as Khorgos at the PRC–Kazakhstan border. Operational and regulatory requirements also require truck to truck transshipment in places such as the Afghanistan–Uzbekistan border, leading to some logistics developments at Termez.[9]

Finally, though border crossings should not necessarily create transport chain breakpoints (i.e., where goods are transshipped from one vehicle to another), they may provide facilities for temporary storage, inspections, and border procedures. At some point these logistics facilities may evolve as gateway platforms, i.e., goods are stored just after a border crossing on customs-bonded warehouses, where they may eventually be distributed within the country or re-exported to third countries.

---

[6] Logistics literature uses a wide variety of terms such as "platform", "hub", and "center" to describe warehouses. Regional distribution centers may be referred to as "regional hubs" and local distribution platforms as "urban distribution centers."

[7] Transshipment between air and rail transport is extremely rare. Typically, air transport moves time-sensitive and high-value goods, while rail cargo is rarely time sensitive nor high value.

[8] Change of gauge can be also achieved without rail-to-tail transshipment by lifting wagons and changing bogies or using wagons with variable axle length.

[9] The information on Afghanistan was collected from international sources.

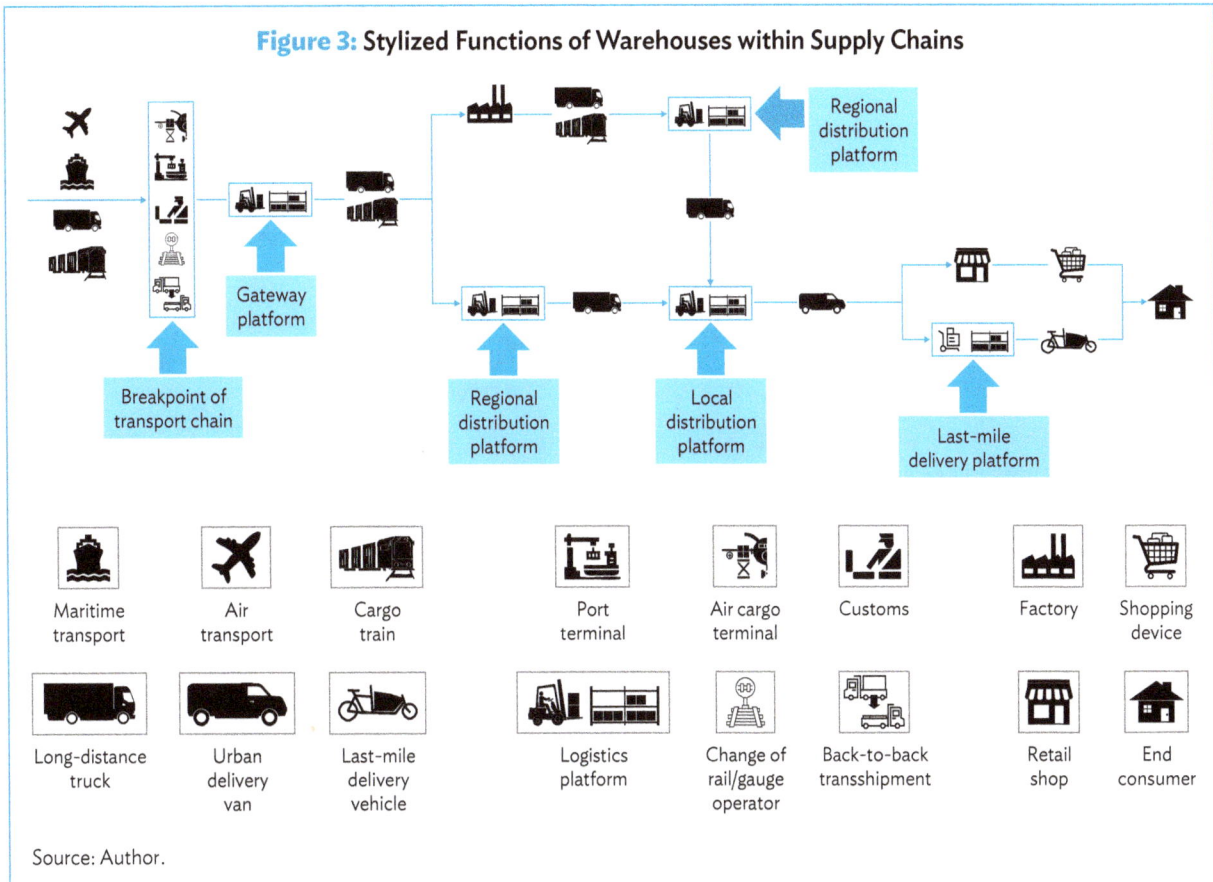

Figure 3: Stylized Functions of Warehouses within Supply Chains

Source: Author.

Breakpoints in transport chains are intrinsically negative in terms of efficiency, reliability, and costs. Hence, artificially created breakpoints, i.e., those not created by technical or operational constraints but for regulatory decisions, should be carefully assessed.

Accordingly, LCs at or beside border crossings may not necessarily be conducive to the creation of efficient transport chains but rather may reflect artificially created inefficiencies. Box 2 describes examples of LCs at borders in CAREC countries.

Box 2: Examples of Logistics Centers at Borders

Border posts house government services, such as immigration, customs, health and quarantine, and phytosanitary controls, and are normally owned and operated by government agencies. Best practice is the so-called one-stop posts, where all involved services are present in one facility, allowing import or export procedures to be processed in a single transaction.

Privately owned warehouses or logistics centers (LCs) involved in foreign trade (most of them not being near borders) need to house on their premises some of these services, on a permanent or temporary basis. Government agencies rarely pay any rent for the facilities they use (such as office space or laboratories), as their presence is mandatory.

Some Central Asia Regional Economic Cooperation countries have developed or are planning LCs near border crossings.

continued on next page

Box 2: continued

Khorgos Eastern Gates

The People's Republic of China (PRC)–Kazakhstan border is a breakpoint of transport chains. For rail, it is due to a technical need to change gauge. For trucks, bilateral transport regulations require it. Though theoretically, PRC drivers are allowed to drive as far as Almaty and Kazakhs as far as Urumchi, very few reach so far, making Khorgos a de facto transshipment point.

The PRC and Kazakhstan have developed special economic zones on both sides of the border. On the Kazakh side, the Khorgos Eastern Gates Special Economic Zone offers an industrial zone of 224 hectares (ha), a logistics zone of 225 ha and a dry port of 129 ha. On the PRC side, a vast industrial and commercial complex has been developed.

Though traffic along the Eurasian corridor has grown steadily and transshipment terminals keep busy, the success of the Khorgos Eastern Gates to attract logistics companies to build warehouses there has been so far limited. In fact, it is Almaty (more than 300 kilometers from Khorgos) that is experiencing logistics developments.

Khorgos Gateway Terminal. Rail transshipment operations in action (photo by author).

Yallama Border Customs Terminal

Uzbekistan has taken an innovative approach under a public–private partnership to create customs and inspection facilities. The concept is that a private partner builds and operates for a period of time a complex that includes facilities for government and commercial use. Areas for government use include offices, customer service areas, bonded warehouses, and rest and changing rooms for government staff. Facilities for commercial use include warehouse space, offices for the private sector (such as customs brokers and banks), a canteen, hotel, and car and truck parking.

This approach is being tested at Yallama Border Customs Terminal, where facilities have been built and are expected to be fully operational in 2022. A similar approach will be tested in Andijan.

continued on next page

Box 2: continued

Yallama Border Customs Terminal. On the left is the one-stop border post, and on the right is the first phase of the warehouse construction—in the foreground is the space used for inspections, while at the back is space used for commercial storage (photos by author).

Yallama LC is located just beside the border post with Kazakhstan on a plot of 20 ha. At first phase, a 5,000 square meter customs warehouse has been built as well as a one-stop border post, requiring a $15 million investment. For the second phase, cold rooms and a hotel are planned.

LCs at border crossings may not necessarily be conductive to more efficient logistics if they are the result of artificially created breakpoints in transport chains. Accordingly, developers such as those of Yallama LC should focus on the ability of all stakeholders (public and private) to offer an attractive value proposition to customers, not on the ability to collect fees from captive customers that need to deal with customs and inspections agencies.

Source: Author's site visits.

Regional distribution platforms

Regional distribution platforms are warehouses where inventory is held to service wide catchment areas. There is no standard definition of the size of a catchment area. Though as an indication, it could be any point within one day's driving distance one way. In small countries one distribution platform may be sufficient for all the country, or it may even happen that a regional distribution platform is located abroad.[10] In bigger countries, the market is served from a variety of regional distribution platforms.

Depending on the company profile, nature of products, and size of catchment area, these warehouses may require extensive storage capacity, meaning that ample land availability is needed. Typically, they have loading docks only on one side as transport operations are less frequent but use bigger trucks.

Local distribution platforms

Local distribution platforms serve as cross-docking points between long haul transport and urban distribution usually servicing retail, hospitality, and businesses in urban or metropolitan areas.

[10] As an example, some warehouses in Almaty operate as regional distribution centers for some cargo bound to the Kyrgyz Republic.

Figure 4: Example of Regional Distribution Platform

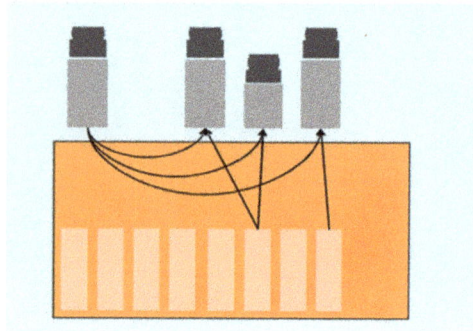

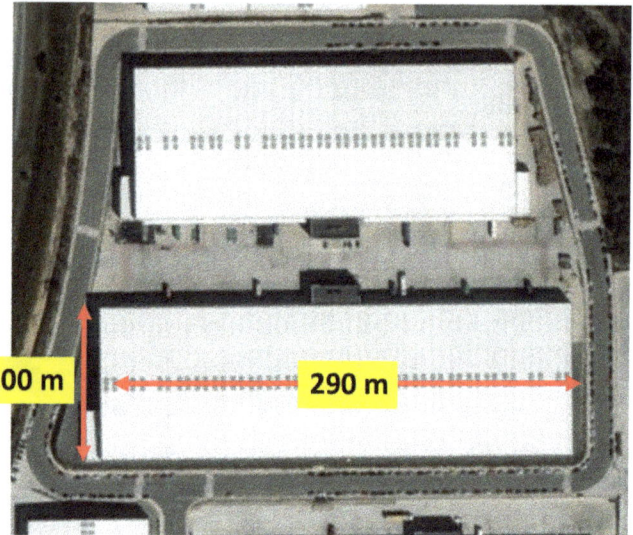

m = meter.

Notes: A sketch of functions is on the left, while on the right is an aerial view of a regional distribution platform. The warehouse width of regional distribution platforms is commonly close to 100 m (diagram by author, photo via open-source map).

These functions are often carried out by wholesalers.[11] A catchment area is usually defined by the distance that can be covered by a small truck or delivery van to serve a variety of customers in at least one daily roundtrip.

These platforms require proximity to large consumption markets and easy access to them so that customers can be serviced by a small truck or van in one or more delivery rounds in a single day. Since their main function is to be cross-docking points, turnaround of goods is quick and there is little need of a storage area, but they tend to have as many loading docks as possible, typically on both long sides. Warehouse width is reduced to shorten internal movements between docks. Internal movements may be made using forklifts or be automated with sorting devices.

In many cities in developing countries, local distribution platforms are in legacy locations such as old wholesale markets that have been encroached upon by urban growth.[12] This situation creates congestion, the circulation of heavy trucks on city roads, and is characterized by operations performed in suboptimal premises. Many early LCs, as described in Appendix 2, appeared as solutions to overcome these situations.

Fulfillment centers. As a result of e-commerce, a new type of facility is emerging to fulfill e-commerce shipments aimed at being delivered in a maximum of one day. Fulfillment centers are basically local distribution centers but differ from them in size (because of the vast number of individual shipments they handle) and customer type, which is end consumers compared to retail and business for local distribution centers.

---

[11] Wholesalers own and sell merchandise. Local distribution platforms may be operated by transport companies or logistics providers that transport and handle goods owned by shippers.

[12] Tbilisi's Eliava market for wholesale building materials is an example.

Figure 5: Example of Local Distribution Platforms

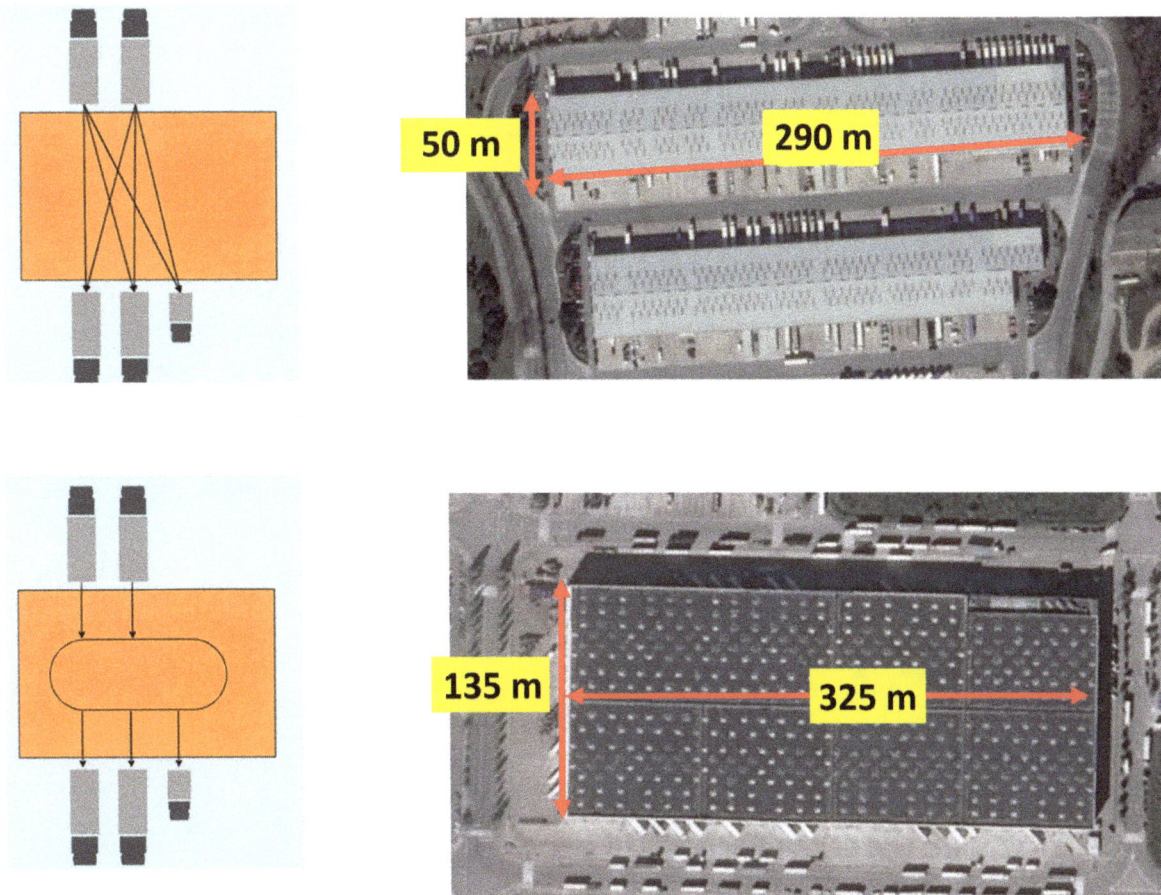

m = meter.

Notes: Sketches on the left illustrate functions of cross-docking platforms. Cross-docking may be made using manual pallet trucks or forklifts (upper left) or automated sorters (lower left). This may have significant impact on the size and form of warehouses as seen in the photos on the right. The upper right figure shows two cross-docking warehouses of transport companies featuring docks on both sides, and width being around 50 m. This is the typical pattern for cross-docking using pallet trucks or forklifts. The lower right figure features the distribution center of a supermarket chain where internal movements are made using an automated sorter. In this case, the warehouse is much wider and features loading docks on three sides (diagrams by author, photos via open-source map).

Last-mile delivery platforms

Last-mile delivery platforms are an emerging type of facility underpinned by the growth of e-commerce and coming in a variety of formats and functions. They may be micro-fulfillment centers catering for "quick-commerce" (i.e., goods delivered in a very short time), or may be transshipment points from vans to smaller vehicles (e.g., bikes and scooters) used in the last-mile delivery of small items. They are normally located in urban areas, even downtown.

Other types of platforms

The above list of platforms and locations is by no means exhaustive. Platforms may be clustered near major factories to deliver just-in-time supplies or to store inventories of finished products. Or they may be in areas growing agricultural produce to consolidate stock for later distribution. In addition, a wide range of specialized logistics, e.g., for fuels, chemicals, minerals, other bulk materials, and fresh produce (Section 3.1.5), that follow specific operational and location patterns do not always match the models already described.

3.1.2 What are intermodal and multimodal platforms?

Intermodal platforms are located at the interface of two modes of transport, such as maritime–road, maritime–rail, air–road, or rail–road. Multimodal platforms are located at the interface of more than two modes, such as maritime–rail–road or road–rail–air. Warehouses at intermodal or multimodal platforms should be as close as possible to transport infrastructure where cargo is handled.[13]

Air cargo centers typically feature two lines: airside and landside. Airside warehouses are designed to cross-dock cargo from aircraft to trucks and need direct access to the apron. Landside warehouses are designed to consolidate air cargo to be eventually shuttled to the airside or sent on a road feeder service.[14] They may also split unit load devices and distribute received cargo.[15]

In ports, warehouses may be on-dock and off-dock. On-dock warehouses are commonly used for bulk and breakbulk cargo. Off-dock warehouses are expected to be as close as possible to terminals to minimize the costs of shuttling cargo from dock to warehouse.

Rail–road intermodal platforms have two main features. Non-containerized breakbulk carried on rail wagons is off-loaded horizontally from doors on one side of them. This operation is often made on warehouses dotted with a rail siding on one side and docks to receive trucks on the opposite side. This is a common pattern in CIS countries, where rail transport still plays a key role in long-distance transport. This feature requires warehouses to be located close to marshaling yards to connect to their rail sidings. Rail transported containers are off-loaded vertically using gantry cranes or reach stackers.

An airside warehouse.
Air Cargo Center Liege, Belgium, has warehouses with direct access to the apron and airfreight handling equipment (photo by author).

---

[13] Details on standards and requirements for combined transport facilities are set at the European Agreement on Important International Combined Transport Lines (AGTC). See UNECE. 2010. European Agreement on Important International Combined Transport Lines and Related Installations (AGTC). Geneva. https://unece.org/DAM/trans/conventn/agtce.pdf; UNECE. 1997. Protocol on Combined Transport on Inland Waterways to the European Agreement on Important International Combined Transport Lines and Related Installations (AGTC) of 1991. Geneva. https://unece.org/DAM/trans/conventn/pro-agtc-e.pdf.

[14] Under a road feeder service, cargo is transported by road to a third airport to be boarded on an airplane for the second leg of its journey, using a single airway bill as proof of transport contract.

[15] Unit load devices are the equivalent of shipping containers for air cargo.

An off-dock logistics center beside a container and rail terminal. London Gateway Logistics Centre is located beside the on-dock container terminal. Between them is a rail line and rail container terminal (photo courtesy of London Gateway).

Warehouses handling containerized rail cargo do not need rail sidings on one side but tend to be as close as possible to the rail terminal to reduce the time and cost of shuttling containers.[16]

3.1.3 What are the most suitable locations?

As a rule of thumb, the most suitable locations for distribution platforms can be deduced by examining the distance–cost equation (Figure 6).

For local distribution platforms, transport costs are critical but little storage area is required so warehouses need not be big. These platforms can therefore choose locations close to major access roads to cities, even though land prices are high.

For regional distribution platforms, the key factor is the availability and cost of land, as warehouses need to be bigger. Accordingly, they may seek locations further away where land is cheaper, but close to major transport corridors or, even better, near crossroads to ensure easy access to their catchment area.

Logistics jargon includes the terms "prime areas," "first ring," and "logistics rings." Prime areas are either very close to freight transport infrastructure, such as ports, or within the "first ring," typically defined as within a radius of 10–20 kilometers from a city, both with good access to major roads. Land prices are high, and these locations are sought by intermodal platforms or local distribution platforms. Regional distribution platforms servicing regional or national markets tend to be in the second or third rings, i.e., within a radius of 20–100 kilometers, depending on the availability of land and size of the market.

---

16   Though still very common in CIS countries, as a general trend breakbulk non-containerized rail cargo seems to be losing market share against rail containers. This is consistent with the evolution in Europe and the Americas, where rail transport of breakbulk is marginal. Having said this, moving breakbulk on wagons may still make robust economic sense in Central Asia due to the long distances involved and the capillarity of the rail network reaching many factories and warehouses. It is worth noting that the re-introduction of rail transport to move small shipments across long distances using consolidation centers is being considered on environmental grounds in some countries.

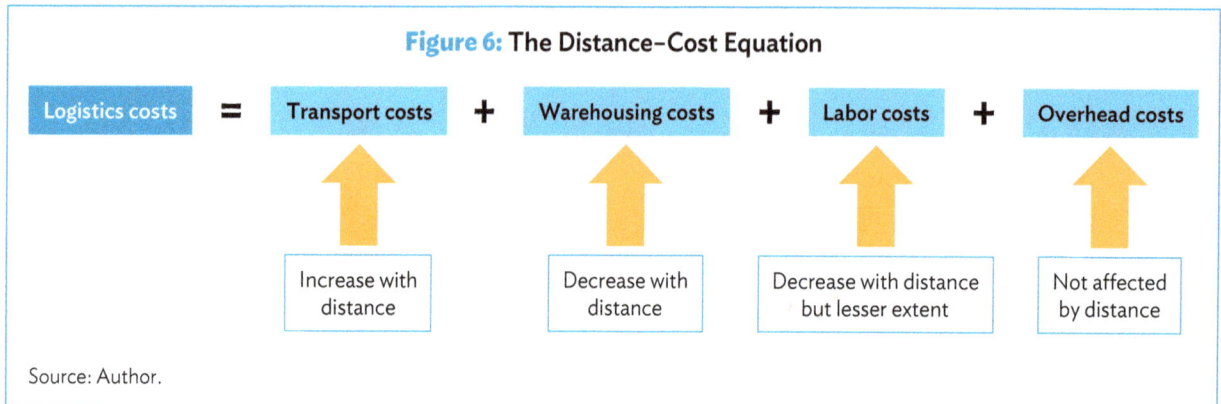

Figure 6: The Distance–Cost Equation

Logistics costs	=	Transport costs	+	Warehousing costs	+	Labor costs	+	Overhead costs
		Increase with distance		Decrease with distance		Decrease with distance but lesser extent		Not affected by distance

Source: Author.

Note that while a longer distance from the city may contribute to lower labor costs, it may reduce the availability of skilled staff.

3.1.4 Are dry ports logistics centers?

Dry ports are inland terminals to which shipping companies can issue import or export bills of lading assuming full responsibility of costs and conditions.[17] Similar functions are performed by inland container depots (ICDs). Dry ports and ICDs can be connected to seaports by rail or inland waterways (so they are intermodal platforms as described above), or by road. Dry ports and ICDs are common in landlocked countries and other large countries with regions distant from the sea.[18]

The Intergovernmental Agreement on Dry Ports signed by most CAREC countries recommends that dry ports include the following:

- a secure area with a gate for dedicated entrance and exit;

- covered and open storage areas separated for import, export, and transshipment, and for perishable goods, high-value cargo, and dangerous cargo, including hazardous substances;
- warehousing facilities, which may include customs bonded warehousing facilities;
- customs supervision, control, inspection, and storage facilities;
- appropriate cargo and container-handling equipment;
- internal service roads and pavements for use in the operation and stacking area;
- vehicle holding areas with adequate parking space for freight vehicles;
- an administrative building for customs, freight forwarders, shippers, customs brokers, banks, and other related agencies;
- information and communications systems, including electronic data interchange systems, scanners, and vehicle-weighing equipment; and
- a container, vehicle, and equipment repair yard, if necessary.[19]

---

17   United Nations Conference on Trade and Development. 1991. *Handbook on the Management and Operations of Dry Ports.* Geneva. https://unctad.org/system/files/official-document/rdpldc7_en.pdf.

18   The European Agreement on Important International Combined Transport Lines (AGTC) also sets some technical and operational parameters for combined transport terminals, though they are quite focused on rail. See UNECE. 2010. European Agreement on Important International Combined Transport Lines and Related Installations (AGTC). Geneva. https://unece.org/DAM/trans/conventn/agtce.pdf.

19   UN Economic and Social Commission for Asia and the Pacific. 2013. *Intergovernmental Agreement on Dry Ports.* https://treaties.un.org/doc/Treaties/2013/11/20131107%2012-02%20PM/XI-E-3.pdf.

These facilities and services are quite similar to what is proposed in this guide for LCs. Thus, it can be assumed that dry ports featuring these characteristics are a kind of LC.

A similar concept is an off-dock terminal used to ferry cargo by truck or train on shorter distances to and from seaports, usually to mitigate congestion around port areas, e.g., ICDs Uiwang and Yangsan for Busan port in the Republic of Korea[20] and ZEAL for Valparaiso port in Chile.[21]

3.1.5 What are the specificities of agricultural produce logistics?

There is a wide range of logistics and value-addition processes for agricultural and farming produce. Meat, dairy products, cereals, and fresh vegetables and fruits require different processing and may follow different distribution channels.

In addition, logistics of produce bound for internal consumption may be quite different from logistics for export commodities. Figure 7 illustrates a simplified model of an agro-produce logistics chain and shows the main players involved.

Aggregation and first processing facilities are likely to be close to production areas. They may be cooperatives (i.e., owned by producers) or owned by third parties as businesses or public sector facilities. As a principle, government policies encourage that value addition, and control of the supply chain is made as close as possible to production areas, e.g., through supporting **agro-centers** providing storage, processing and trading facilities, and other services to promote technologies, skills, marketing, and so on.

Bulk traders typically handle supplies for big buyers (e.g., the food industry, the government through strategic stocks schemes, or export markets) and have substantial storage capacity capable of accommodating

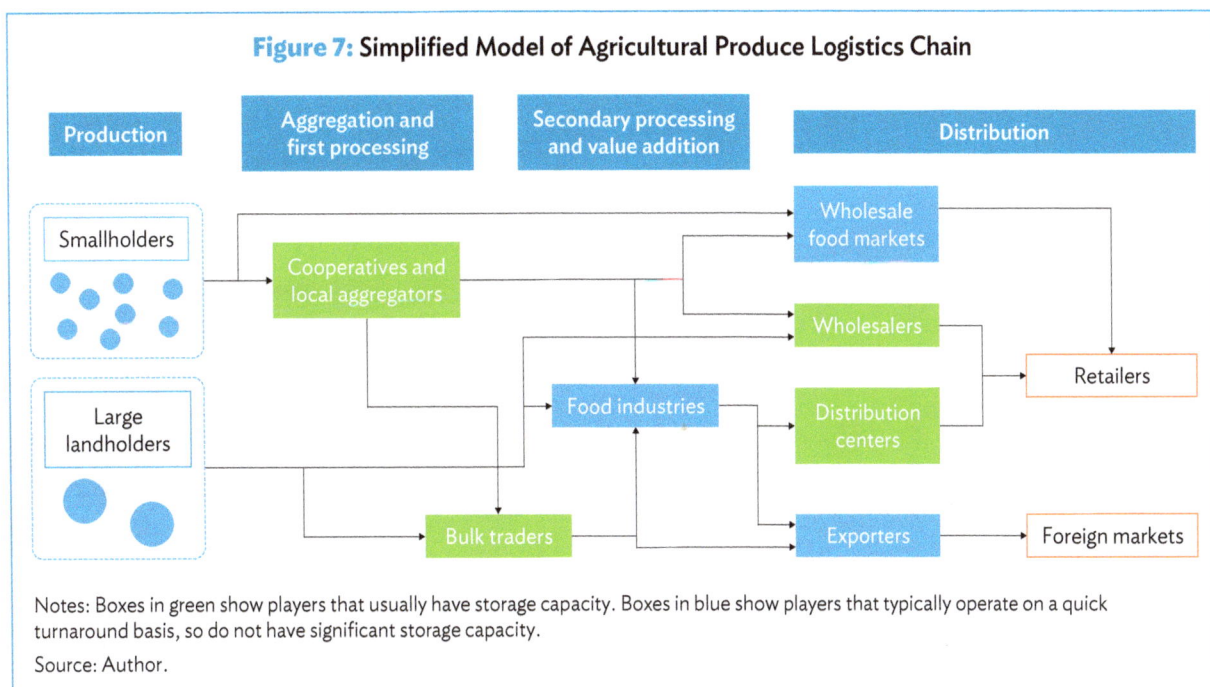

Figure 7: Simplified Model of Agricultural Produce Logistics Chain

Notes: Boxes in green show players that usually have storage capacity. Boxes in blue show players that typically operate on a quick turnaround basis, so do not have significant storage capacity.
Source: Author.

20   J. D. Park, J. S. Jo, and G. S. Kim. 2017. *Inland Container Depot (ICD) in Korea: Focusing on Uiwang and Yangsan.* Korea Maritime Institute.

21   ZEAL is an off-dock terminal linked to the harbor through an underground tunnel across the city of Valparaiso. See ZEAL Puerto Valparaiso. https://www.zeal.cl/.

stocks between producing seasons and sometimes beyond them. Big warehouses or silos will be typically located near transport infrastructure capable of moving great volumes (e.g., rail, inland waterways, and trunk roads).

Distribution in local markets may be carried out by wholesalers or distribution centers. Their functions can be assimilated into local distribution centers as described in Section 3.1.1.

Wholesale food markets serving major cities or agglomerations are a specific type of local distribution platform. In many cities, municipal authorities have promoted these facilities to concentrate both wholesalers and direct sales from local producers to retailers.[22] A trend in many cities has been the relocation of these markets from inner-city sites to suburban locations where accessibility and food safety conditions can be improved. In fact, these relocations have been at the origin of some LCs (e.g., Sogaris, Appendix 2). In Azerbaijan, Meyveli Bazaar is an example of a private sector-led wholesale food market (Appendix 1).

3.2 Conceptual Design and Layout

3.2.1 How can the right size and functions of a logistics center be assessed?

A key issue when planning an LC is the expected functions of companies that are to be attracted. Potential market in terms of size and type of companies should stem from market studies assessing both potential demand as well as the existing and planned supply of industrial land.

An LC need not be homogeneous, i.e., focus only on one of the functions described in the previous section. These functions are stylized models—in practice, each company may have its particular needs and operational characteristics. However, the predominant type of logistics functions will be closely related to location and will influence the size, layout, and eventually the commercial model.

Regarding size, there is no rule of thumb. However, small developments of less than 20 ha may not have sufficient critical mass to generate synergies among companies nor fund some shared services, as will be described in Section 4.2.4. It is advisable to choose locations with potential for scaling up development in various stages.

3.2.2 What differentiates the layout of a logistics center from a conventional industrial park?

Access roads. As LCs are expected to generate intense flows of trucks, those focused on distribution close to cities in particular need to have access roads and a connection to the main road network that is robust, with their design based on mobility studies looking ahead to when the LC will be fully developed. When possible, it is wise to plan more than one way of access in case one is disrupted. Access roads should be designed to support intense traffic of heavy vehicles, so for instance avoiding sharp bends, steep gradients, and left turns.

Orthogonal layout. Warehouses tend to be rectangles. This form optimizes the internal space for transshipment and to accommodate storage racks and fulfillment areas. To offer the highest value to potential customers, LC developers should plan their layouts so that resulting plots of land have a rectangular pattern. Marginal spaces may be dedicated to other uses, e.g., car or truck parks, yards, and technical facilities.

---

22   The World Union of Wholesale Markets is an international organization representing wholesale food markets. https://wuwm.org/about/.

Example of an orthogonal layout with access road. At Clesud Logistics Center in Miramas, France, a high-capacity roundabout connects the main road to the LC, as well as the rectangular pattern of plots (photo via open-source maps).

Internal roads. Efficient internal mobility is a key requirement for an LC's success. Typically, an internal road system will have a hierarchical structure consisting of an arterial network and a secondary network. The arterial network is the main access and distribution road system and forms the backbone of the LC's layout. It should facilitate free movement at a relatively fluid speed; thus, left turns should be avoided, except with roundabouts, and trucks should not be allowed to park along its sides. The arterial network is not intended to provide direct access to plots. This system may have a grid or branched pattern. The secondary network consists of lanes providing access to plots and other facilities from the arterial network.

In an LC, the area dedicated to internal roads may be substantial, indicatively 15%–20% of gross surface area, which is usually above the ratio in conventional industrial areas. Moreover, when designing the layout, it can be smart to anticipate where warehouses may have loading docks on both sides so as to provide access roads to both sides of the plot as well.

Qualities and width of internal roads may need to follow standards regulated by concerned authorities. However, it is recommended to have a minimum lane width of 3.5–3.75 m to allow fluid movement of vehicles. Reinforced pavements to avoid rapid wear and tear from intense use by heavy vehicles is also recommended.

Left turns may complicate fluidity of movement. Roundabouts should be designed to allow easy turns by heavy goods vehicles, i.e., have an outside radius of greater than 25 m.

Gradients. Logistics plots require an almost horizontal longitudinal profile and minimal height differences with the secondary access roads. In case of uneven or sloping terrains, gradients should be kept to the arterial network and in any case excessive gradients (i.e., greater than 3%–3.5%) should be avoided.

Plot form and size. This is another key success factor for an LC. While form and size may be predetermined up to a point by the internal road structure, some flexibility so as to accommodate customers with different needs in terms of plot size and type of platform should be included.

The type of plot customization shown in the photo above is typical of LCs where plots are intended to be sold. However, LCs designed to rent warehouse space have a more homogenous pattern. In these cases, it is riskier to customize warehouses that will accommodate a variety of customers during their lifetime. Flexibility in these cases is offered in terms of different types of warehouse width and by the construction of modular warehouses that can be segmented to accommodate various companies of different size under the same roof.

Securitization. Controlled access and security are added values for LCs as they reduce the risk of pilferage and insurance costs. Controlled access gates, perimeter fences, surveillance cameras, and control centers are capital costs usually not borne by developers of conventional industrial parks.

Figure 8: Example of Flexibility of Plot Form and Size

The arterial roads in Plaza LC, Zaragoza, Spain, define "superblocks." Superblock #1 has been allocated to a single client that built a vast consolidation platform. Superblock #2 includes one horizontal secondary road and accommodates medium-sized companies, the two on the lower part featuring warehouses with considerable width (around 150 m) and the ones on the upper part featuring around 50 m of warehouse width. Superblock #3 has one vertical and three horizontal secondary roads and has been sliced to accommodate small and medium platforms. Superblock #4 has two horizontal secondary roads and seems conceived to accommodate medium-sized platforms. Finally, the internal structure of superblock #5 has not been totally defined yet and could either accommodate a vast platform or smaller ones (photo via open-source maps, with author's additions).

Intermodal and service areas. Apart from warehouses, LCs may have a variety of functional areas such as rail terminals, containers yards, truck parks, yards for bulk materials, fuel stations, service and rest areas, service centers, hotels, commercial buildings, and amenities for workers and visitors. Ideally these should provide synergies and added value to companies located in the LC and may become sources of ancillary revenue to the LC developer.

3.2.3 What other land planning parameters are recommended?

LCs may target different types of users so it is hard to recommend one-size-fits-all land planning parameters, though some general recommendations may be proposed:

Minimum size of plots. LCs targeting small transport companies may set lower thresholds than those targeting big logistics operators. Considering that around 30%, if not more, of the plot will not be built to leave room for loading, maneuvering, and parking areas, a reasonable minimum threshold is 5,000 square meters (m²), which will allow to build up to 3,000 m² approximately. Companies needing a smaller covered surface would be better accommodated in integrated modular warehouses as described in Section 3.3.3.

Plot width. When setting minimum thresholds for plot width, it should be considered that around 18–20 m will be required for loading and maneuvering areas in their front, and a setback from the plot's edge of around 10 m is recommended to allow for emergency access in their back.

Floor area/plot surface ratio. The ratio of floor area to plot surface indicates the proportion of the warehouse footprint over the total plot surface. Since warehouses need to leave open space for trucks at loading docks and setbacks from the plot's edge, a ratio of 0.6 may be sufficient.

Multiple-level warehouses are being built, though their construction is expensive and their operation is complex, so they are only affordable in extremely congested metropolitan areas.

3.2.4 Do LC specificities, compared with industrial parks, have an impact on costs and profitability?

Yes. Developing an LC may be more expensive than developing a conventional industrial park and can be less profitable. First let's look at costs. LCs may be more costly to develop for several reasons:

- Land prices in strategic and well-connected locations tend to be high.
- More expensive infrastructure is required to ensure fluid and intense movement of heavy vehicles.
- Earthworks are needed to ensure orthogonal structure and suitable gradients.
- They have a denser network of internal roads.
- Other infrastructure and facilities, e.g., rail infrastructure, truck parks, service areas, and security, is required.

Then, let us look at revenue. Revenue from LCs may be less than from industrial parks for these reasons:

- More land dedicated to internal roads results in less land available for marketable plots.
- Land dedicated to associated infrastructure and facilities, such as yards and truck parks, has lower market value.
- Similarly, warehouses need to have yards for trucks at loading docks as well as buffer space for maneuvers. Less built area in a plot means less marketable floor space.
- Most LCs restrict acceptable activities (i.e., transport and logistics companies and associated services), so the pool of potential customers is smaller than for industrial parks without such restrictions.

- Transport and logistics typically work with very thin margins and strong competition; thus, it is very sensitive to land prices and rents.

The combination of higher costs and lower revenue explains why private sector developers may perceive LCs as riskier and less remunerative than conventional industrial parks, especially in places where this concept is still a novelty and potential customers have little awareness of their advantages.

3.2.5 What types of companies should logistics centers target?

Conventional industrial parks may host a large range of activities, from any kind of manufacturing to transport, storage, wholesalers, retailers, repair workshops, hotels, and so on. LCs, on the other hand, are designed to accommodate the needs of transport and logistics,

so they may set some regulations in their master plans to restrict acceptable activities. Activities other than transport and logistics may not only dilute the purpose of the LC but also discourage their targeted users.

However, transport and logistics is increasingly becoming a more complex industry as companies engage progressively in integrated solutions, including value-added activities. Manufacturers used to outsource separately transport, freight forwarding, and storage to specialized companies. Currently, these activities are integrated in third-party logistics providers and even fourth-party logistics providers that include other value-added activities such as order preparations, labelling, components assembling, and packaging. This evolution is illustrated in Figure 9.

Accordingly, master plan regulations should be flexible so these value-added logistics can be considered acceptable activities within the LC.

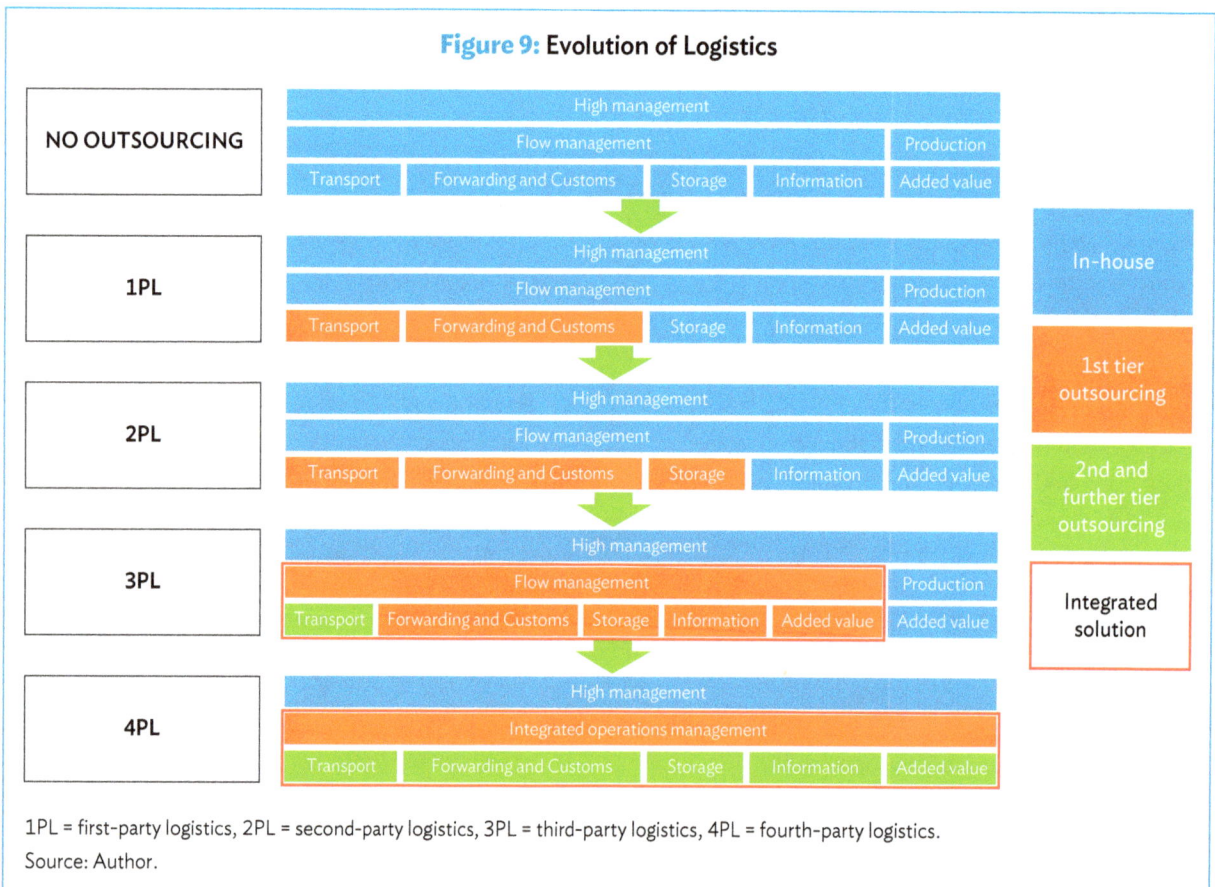

Figure 9: Evolution of Logistics

1PL = first-party logistics, 2PL = second-party logistics, 3PL = third-party logistics, 4PL = fourth-party logistics.
Source: Author.

3.3 Warehouses

3.3.1 How do functions influence warehouse characteristics?

Turnaround of cargo is the key aspect that influences warehouse characteristics. Platforms designed for high turnaround, i.e., where there is only cross-docking and little or no inventory is kept, have many loading docks and less or even no storage area. General recommendations for **high turnaround platforms** are that they should have:

- a warehouse depth of less than 45–50 m;
- an internal layout as open as possible, with a minimum number of columns to allow forklifts to move freely around;
- a maximum number of loading docks on the façade, sometimes on both main façades; and
- a height clearance not below 7–10 m in anticipation of long-term need of racks or handling equipment.

At the other extreme, platforms with low turnaround intended to consolidate cargo and keep inventories will need fewer loading docks and more storage area. General recommendations for **low turnaround platforms** are that they should have:

- a warehouse width of around 100 m for safety purposes, so that emergency exits are at a maximum of 50 m, though wider warehouses may require more sophisticated fire protection systems, which make them more expensive;
- a reception/dispatch area where shipments are received or prepared measuring around 20–25 m width in front of each dock;
- an internal height clearance generally 12–14 m or more, though some warehouses dotted with automated storage systems may have 18–20 m or more; and
- Loading docks may be in one or both sides though the rate of docks per 1,000 m^2 is lower than in high turnaround platforms.

Warehouse reception/dispatching area. The reception/dispatch area in a warehouse with cargo prepared for dispatching on the right (photo by author).

These are simplified recommendations, and LC planners should be aware of potential customers' needs and operational practices, and allow for flexibility in regulations and building parameters to adapt to particular circumstances.

3.3.2 What should Class A and Class B warehouses feature?

Logistics developers and real estate agents sometimes refer to Class A, B, or C warehouses—Class A being a proxy for top standard. It is to be noted that there is no universally accepted definition of the characteristics and standards of Class A, B, or C warehouses, though some common features in the product definition of Class A warehouses can be described as follows:

- minimum internal clearance height of 10 m;
- same level surface at all points in the warehouse;
- minimum floor carrying capacity of 5 tons (t);
- minimum one dock per 1,000 m²;
- building frame allowing minimum clear space between columns of around 240 m²;
- truck maneuvering area of at least 32 m (that may include roads);
- indoor lighting with a minimum of 150 lux;

- area for order preparation and fulfillment (20 m), free of columns;
- fire extinguishing system compliant to local regulations and nonflammable insulation; and
- battery-charging facility for forklifts and handling equipment.

Some of the listed features of Class A warehouses (e.g., clearance height and floor carrying capacity) make less sense for cross-docking platforms with little, if any, storage activity.

From a purely business viewpoint, Class A warehouses have long-term logic. As warehouses may have lifetimes stretching beyond 30 years, developers with a long-term view may anticipate demands of more sophisticated logistics operations.

Class A warehouses may be beyond the possibilities and needs of some transport and logistics players in CAREC countries. Efficient Class B warehouses might be defined as having some but not all of the above conditions, e.g., an internal clearance of 7.5 m, floor carrying capacity of 3 t, one dock per 1,500 m², etc. Class C warehouses may be described as those not fulfilling the standards of Class A nor B.

Class A and Class B warehouses. On the left, the Sapa Logistics Class A warehouse in Astana features an internal height of 12 m and goods are stacked on racks. On the right, a Class B warehouse in Córdoba (Argentina), features an internal height of 7.5 m and goods are stacked on the ground (photos by author).

As an example of what is already being done in the region, Box 3 summarizes Kazakhstan's guidelines for warehouses at LCs.

Box 3: Kazakhstan's Guidelines for Warehouses at Logistics Centers

The standard requirements for transport and logistics centers in Kazakhstan (see Box 1) sets some technical standards for warehouses summarized as

- a one-story warehouse building, preferably rectangular;
- smooth concrete floor with anti-dust coating, with carrying capacity of at least 5 tons/square meter (m^2) and the floor elevated 1.20 m from the ground;
- minimum internal clearance height of 8 m;
- adjustable temperature;
- availability of a sufficient number of loading and unloading gates (at least 1 per 500 m^2).
- ventilation system;
- ramp for unloading vehicles;
- availability of sites for parking and maneuvering heavy vehicles;
- availability of auxiliary premises including toilets, showers, utility rooms, and locker rooms for staff; and
- for international centers, dedicated space for temporary storage.

Source: Executive Order of Kazakhstan's Ministry for Investment and Development dated 28 May 2015.

3.3.3 What are modular warehouses?

Some companies prefer to design and build their own platforms to suit their specific operations, standards, and external image.[23] They can build on purchased or leased plots.

However, many companies may not wish to engage in building, may require less surface area, or may prefer to rent already-built facilities rather than purchasing them. Modular warehouses are conceived so that they can be easily sliced by internal walls to accommodate various customers. Multi-client modular warehouses are also popular for developers whose core business is rental, as it provides flexibility to accommodate clients with different space needs during the building lifetime.

Commercial modules may be about 1,000 m^2 (approximately 20 m façade x 50 m depth) for high turnaround platforms through to 2,000–2,500 m^2 for low turnaround platforms.

Some modular warehouses may be designed with smaller modules of approximately 500 m^2 targeted to small and local companies and may not have elevated loading docks.

3.3.4 How should loading docks and maneuvering areas be designed?

Docks should be elevated from the outside platform in a way that seamless horizontal movement from the warehouse floor into a truck's box can be made using handling equipment (e.g., forklifts). Typically, elevation from the ground outside is around 1.2 m for docks designed for heavy trucks and semitrailers and around 0.9 m if docks are designed for light trucks and vans. Small variations may be solved by hydraulic levelers fitted at docks.

Elevated docks require that the warehouse floor is set above the outside ground, which can be achieved by lifting the warehouse through earthworks or pillars, which adds to construction costs.

---

[23] It is increasingly common that international logistics companies avoid building and owning property. Rather, they make long-term rental agreements with developers prepared to engage in the construction and finance of "build-to-suit" warehouses. These operations are also known as turnkey developments.

When the warehouse is not elevated, loading areas may have a gradient toward the building. This poses safety risks as cargo may slip or fall toward staff operating from the dock. It is also counter-indicated for good drainage, because loading areas should be almost flat, though with a slight gradient toward the road where drainage infrastructure should be.

Width of loading areas in front of docks is related to vehicle length. For articulated trucks (trailers) of 16.5 m length, parking areas should measure around 18 m and some additional maneuvering space should be allowed. It is quite common to use roads servicing two opposite warehouses for maneuvering to optimize the use of land, though this may not be a good idea if these roads have intense traffic.

To reduce parking area width, some warehouses feature loading docks angled at less than 90 degrees, e.g., 45 degrees. This slightly reduces the number of available docks on the façade.

3.3.5 How should office space be designed?

As a rule of thumb, office space in logistics platforms is not above 10%–20% of the total floor area. However, warehouse developers should assess carefully their potential customers' needs in terms of size and visibility as well. Some operators may find basic offices sufficient while others, in particular when hosting company headquarters, will prefer more visible premises.

Offices tend to be placed in a way to maximize space for loading docks. A popular solution is offices in a mezzanine (one or two levels) along the entire length of the façade with simple access from the ground floor and offering full visibility of operations inside the warehouse. Sometimes offices are built as an inserted multiple floor building, usually on sides or corners, but also in the middle. Designs combining both models are also possible.

Figure 10: Example of Parking and Maneuvering Area

This transshipment warehouse in CIM la Selva, Spain, features a loading area 18 meters (m) wide (on the left) designed for trailer trucks. They have a total maneuvering area of 30 m using the two-lane, single-direction access road, including a pedestrian path. On the right, loading areas designed for light trucks are 10 m wide, too short for a semitrailer parked on the wrong side, as shown (photo courtesy of CIMALSA, author's additions).

Docks and loading areas. On the left, Continental Logistics Astana has a warehouse with ample maneuvering area at its front to provide sufficient space for trucks, and docks are aligned with the façade; at ALG Logistics in Almaty, warehouses have limited space between them, and docks are angled so as to require less maneuvering area; and on the right, this warehouse in Zona Franca del Pacífico, Colombia, is not elevated from the ground, so the approach to the dock has a negative gradient (photos by author).

Examples of office space in warehouses. On the left, office space is designed as a multistorey inserted building at Logistics Park Rivesaltes, France, with one located on one side (foreground) and another in the middle (background left); on the right, mezzanine offices are set above the operational area at Prologis Maasvlakte, in Rotterdam, the Netherlands (photos by author).

3.3.6 What are the specificities and costs involved in cold storage?

Temperature control may simply involve avoidance of extreme temperatures inside warehouses, e.g., not higher that 40 degrees Celsius and not below 10 degrees Celsius. These limits may also be set to ensure comfortable working conditions for staff or because of the temperature requirements of goods. As weather conditions may be extreme is some CAREC countries, this is a relevant issue. To avoid extremes, warehouses may have heating and cooling systems and strip curtains at gates and docks, or separations between certain areas.

Cold rooms, either positive (above zero) or negative (below zero), are storage areas intended to keep and handle perishables (e.g., food, flowers) and other temperature-sensitive goods such as pharmaceuticals. Cold rooms require additional insulation within warehouses, dedicated freezing devices, and even back-up power generators when energy supply is unreliable. Cold rooms involve high investment and operational costs, in particular for energy as well as specific operational and safety procedures.

3.3.7 How can a rail terminal be integrated into a logistics center?

Conceptually, a rail terminal includes the following elements:

(i) **A spur to connect to the main line.** The technical parameters and operational conditions for connection will need to be discussed and approved by the railway authority.

(ii) **A marshaling yard.** It should comprise enough tacks to perform the following functions:

- Change of traction. As a rule of thumb, the railways operator will move wagons up to the marshaling yard and leave. From here, wagons will be moved by terminal locomotives. Terminal locomotives need to be diesel powered, as catenaries are incompatible with vertical lifting of cargo.
- Split/formation of trains, classification of wagons, and temporary storage of wagons.

(iii) **Loading and unloading areas.** Different types of cargo require different handling equipment and infrastructure. Normally terminals allocate specific areas to handle different cargo.

- Containers are vertically lifted using gantry cranes or reach stackers and deposited in the container yard. Gantry cranes are more expensive but allow more efficient operations and reach a wider number of tracks.
- Iron, steel, and other heavy cargo is usually vertically lifted, and their operation is similar to containers.
- Breakbulk wagons may be unloaded using forklifts. This is a horizontal operation that requires the terminal ground to be level with wagon doors. Often cargo is deposited in closed warehouses adjacent to the tracks.
- Cars are driven from wagons to yards through ramps.
- Trucks and semitrailers may use a variety of systems—from moving on their own onto the platforms, to being vertically lifted.

- The most common wagons for solid bulk are hoppers that are loaded and unloaded using conveyors.

(iv) **Truck circuit.** This should include a controlled gate to allow only authorized trucks in, areas for drivers to wait for their slot to pick up cargo and clear administrative procedures, and an in-and-out itinerary aiming to avoid crossing rail trucks as well as loading and unloading areas.

(v) **Storage areas.** Only cargo expected to have a quick turnaround are kept at the loading and unloading yards, otherwise these are moved to storage areas farther away. Empty container yards are common features in rail terminals. Storage areas may use large portions of land. Terminal managers tend to charge deposit fees to encourage quick turnaround.

(vi) **Communications, safety, and security infrastructure.** The terminal needs to be connected to the rail network to grant safe movements in and out of the main line. It is advisable that rail and road networks are kept as separate as possible and that level crossings are adequately signed and protected. Rail terminals are subject to rail safety regulations and often are customs bonded, thus becoming closed precincts where only authorized vehicles and people are permitted. This explains why LC layouts tend to separate rail terminals from other logistics areas, except when warehouses have rail docks.

Rail terminals require large areas of land, high capital expenditure investment, approvals from railway authorities, and involve significant operational costs. Some LC developers may be hesitant to face these challenges, in particular at the early phases of development when volumes are still small or not consolidated yet. It is advisable that whenever possible LCs are designed in a way to enable the integration of rail transport at some stage of their development, meaning that they reserve the land needed for rail lines, terminals, and yards. In many countries, governments provide some financial support in the context of green transport policies. An example of a rail–road LC is described in Box 4.

Box 4: Damu Logistics Center

Damu Logistics is one of the pioneers in the introduction of the concept of logistics centers (LCs) in Central Asia. The company is at the same time a provider of logistics services and an LC developer and manager.

Damu Industrial Complex near Almaty covers 210 hectares (ha) and started operations in 2004.

The complex comprises three sub-areas:

(i)   a logistics area comprising 110,000 square meters of warehouses built and owned by Damu Logistics. Most warehouses have direct rail access. Damu Logistics operates most of this warehouse capacity but also rents parts to other companies;

(ii) a rail container terminal on 18 ha and operated by Damu Logistics, which also owns two terminal locomotives; and

(iii) an industrial park in the remaining area, where most plots have been sold to a variety of manufacturing, logistics, and services companies. This area has a few examples of turnkey logistics developments (i.e., warehouses built by a developer to suit a specific customer committed to remain as tenant for a period), which are still uncommon in Central Asia.

The complex features a service center including office space for rent, security, heating, a truck park, waste management, snow removal, and an on-site fire brigade.

According to Damu Logistics, it has invested $100 million in the complex and triggered $326 million of investment from other resident companies. Currently, the company is working to develop other LCs in Kazakhstan and abroad.

Damu Industrial and Logistics Complex. Damu container terminal is in the foreground, operated by gantry cranes. Damu Logistics warehouses are the gray-roofed buildings. Rail sidings to the back of most warehouses are used for rail transported breakbulk, marked with blue arrows. On the left of the terminal is a container yard, while the truck park can be observed at the upper right, and the industrial area can be seen in the upper left part of the photo with more heterogeneous buildings (photo courtesy of Damu Logistics, with author's additions).

Sources: Author's site visit; company presentations; and Damu Logistics website (https://dlg.kz/en/about).

3.3.8 How can "green" warehouses be built?

The way warehouses are built and operated can have a significant environmental impact. A variety of measures can be adopted to reduce the environmental footprint of a warehouse, such as

- a design and orientation that optimizes use of daylight, with skylights above corridors between rows of racks;
- utilizing low-energy lighting and equipment, e.g., LED lights, and using sensors to monitor energy consumption;
- insulating against extreme weather conditions;
- using recycled and recyclable building materials whenever possible;
- avoiding toxic paints and adhesives and using wood and other natural products to improve indoor air quality;
- installing solar panels on rooftops; and
- reducing consumption of nonrenewable products, and reusing and recycling materials, e.g., pallets, cardboard, and plastics.

Some organizations provide technical guidelines and advice to improve environmental standards for buildings such as the World Green Building Council and the BRE Foundation.[24]

3.4 Other Infrastructure

3.4.1 What network infrastructure is required at a logistics center?

Network infrastructure is usually similar to what is required in a conventional industrial park:

- **Water.** Water consumption in LCs tend to be relatively low, as typically no manufacturing processes require large amounts of water.

- **Drainage.** As LCs tend to be flat places with vast paved surfaces, efficient drainage is paramount. Often, LCs need rainwater basins to avoid flooding during heavy rains. As pavement may be soiled with lubricants, fuel, or plastics, it is prudent to have some sort of treatment before releasing drained water to the environment.
- **Power.** Medium- and low-voltage electricity supply is essential. Consumption will depend on the automation of handling processes and the use of electric vehicles and handling equipment. On average, a power supply of 50 watts per m^2 may suffice for a standard and not very automated logistics platform.
- **Gas.** In some countries, compressed natural gas is common for powering transport vehicles. Except in these cases, LCs typically have low gas consumption other than for heating.
- **Telecommunications.** Fiber-optic communication and the ability to connect with a variety of telecom providers is paramount.
- **Heating.** Boilers for shared use among various warehouses and buildings is common in some CAREC countries.

When designing an LC, it is prudent to include an underground service gallery to facilitate laying connections to utilities and telecom providers with minimal disruption to the logistics operations.

3.4.2 What other infrastructure is recommended?

Other recommended infrastructure include:

- **Truck parks.** Common in LCs, truck parks provide secure stopovers for trucks on long-distance routes and parking space for trucks owned by resident companies and individual owners. When designing a truck park, it is recommended to forecast which of these two functions will

---

24   World Green Building Council. https://worldgbc.org/; and BREEAM. https://www.breeam.com/.

predominate as management and associated services may differ. Some LCs provide separate parking areas for conventional trucks and for those carrying hazardous materials.

- **Car parks.** Parking areas for cars and trucks should be carefully separated so that cars avoid interfering with truck routes.
- **Security infrastructure.** This includes controlled access gates, a perimeter fence, control cameras, and control center.
- **Lighting.** This should be provided along common-use roads.
- **A fire extinguishing system.** This should include deposits and hydrants as shared infrastructure.
- **Emergency alarm systems.** These are particularly important when hazardous materials are expected to be handled in the complex.
- **Public transport stations.** These facilitate accessibility for staff.
- **Yards.** These can be used for storage of empty containers or breakbulk commodities. As revenue from yards tend to be low, developers often relegate them to marginal pieces of land.
- **Waste management and disposal infrastructure.**

3.4.3 What are service centers?

Service centers offer office and commercial space for complementary and synergic services to logistics companies operating in an LC. Those taking the spaces may include

- the LC administration;
- forwarders, insurance companies, lawyers, accounting companies, interim work agencies, and IT providers;
- government offices such as customs, inspection authorities, and port/rail offices;
- training facilities and meeting and conference rooms; and
- shared services, e.g., mail and parcel reception, control center, and data center.

Examples of service centers. From top to bottom: The service center at Damu, Kazakhstan, which includes company headquarters, offices for rent to third companies, and some services for staff; the service center at Nuremberg Freight Village, Germany, which includes a single window to process intermodal road–rail paperwork; Termez LC, Uzbekistan, which offers convenience stores, accommodation services, offices for rent, and a fuel station; and Highway LC, Uzbekistan, which offers a wide range of services including repair workshops, vehicle dealers, and truck cleaning, located outside the precinct for customers (photos by author, except the second image from the bottom, courtesy of Termez Cargo).

Service centers may also include other amenities such as convenience stores, cafeterias, restaurants, and hotels. These amenities may attract customers beyond LC staff, users, and visitors and may be located outside the fenced perimeter of the LC with an independent access to avoid interference with the operations of the LC.

3.5 Summary

Table 2 summarizes five principles to consider when creating the layout of a logistics center.

Table 2: Five Principles to Inspire the Layout of a Logistics Center

Efficiency	All layout aspects must be conducive to the efficient operations of companies and users operating in the LC: • The location should be well connected, with easy access to main transport corridors. • Roads should be built for the easy movement of vehicles, taking into account capacity, bends, gradients, etc. • Maneuvering and parking areas should be sufficient.
Flexibility	The layout should be flexible, enabling any future adaptations that may be required due to changes in the logistics industry and to accommodate unanticipated demands. This means considering • layout and size of plots; • development in stages; and • regulations that ensure the initial purpose is not diluted while not becoming unnecessarily rigid either.
Optimization	The layout should optimize the use of space by • avoiding under-using space; • looking for valuable uses of marginal spaces; and • designing open, green areas to provide positive impacts to the landscape and environment.
Marketability	The LC should be designed to respond to the real needs of potential customers, be financially feasible, and ensure long-term sustainability. This means • designing attractive value proposition; • identifying most profitable areas/activities to offset least profitable ones; and • avoiding unnecessary constraints on and cumbersome procedures for potential customers.
Governance	LC design should be consistent with future governance and operations: • From conception, it should be clear who will oversee operating and maintaining all pieces of land, infrastructure, and facilities. • The conceptual design of the LC should anticipate the governance of the complex.

LC = logistics center.
Source: Author.

4

PROJECT PREPARATION, IMPLEMENTATION, AND OPERATIONS

4.1 Road Map to Implementation

4.1.1 What steps are required to implement a logistics center?

A road map is summarized in Figure 11, and is similar to other transport infrastructure projects. However, some particularities need to be clearly understood from the beginning:

- the variety of concerned stakeholders, often with limited understanding of what LCs are, and sometimes with conflicting interests;
- the fact that LCs need to attract customers, i.e., transport and logistics companies; and
- the need to create a vehicle to implement the project and manage it in a commercial manner.

4.1.2 What stakeholders may be involved?

Involved stakeholders will evolve as the LC project progresses through implementation stages, as will the nature of the leading actor, from sponsor, then developer, and finally to operator as is illustrated in Figure 12. The nature, functions, and risks of this leading actor are described in Section 4.2.

Key stakeholders at launching stage are line ministries, in particular those dealing with transport infrastructure, planning, and public works.

Port, railway, or airport authorities are crucial to ensure connectivity and operational capacity at intermodal LCs. In some countries, port or railway authorities may have substantial political and financial clout matching those of some line ministries. For their part, sector stakeholders and industry groups will pursue their specific and individual interests. A major challenge at launching stage is that most concerned parties may not have a clear notion about the concept and specificities of LCs, especially in countries where there is no example to serve as a reference. Sharing information and examples from other places may be useful to achieve informed and meaningful discussions.

Key actors at implementation stage are those involved in the approval procedures of engineering designs and master plan. Approvals and implementation may be challenged by affected groups. Of paramount importance are landowners and settled people and businesses. It should be noted that not only is land being secured a necessary condition, but also that land prices may challenge the feasibility of an LC project. Social groups may also be concerned about environmental and socioeconomic impacts of an LC. Some arguments to address these concerns are discussed in Section 5. LC planning approvals can be streamlined when developed on public domain land, or on land owned and managed by port, airport, or railway authorities.

Attention should be paid to potential customers and competitors, as an LC is a commercial endeavor.

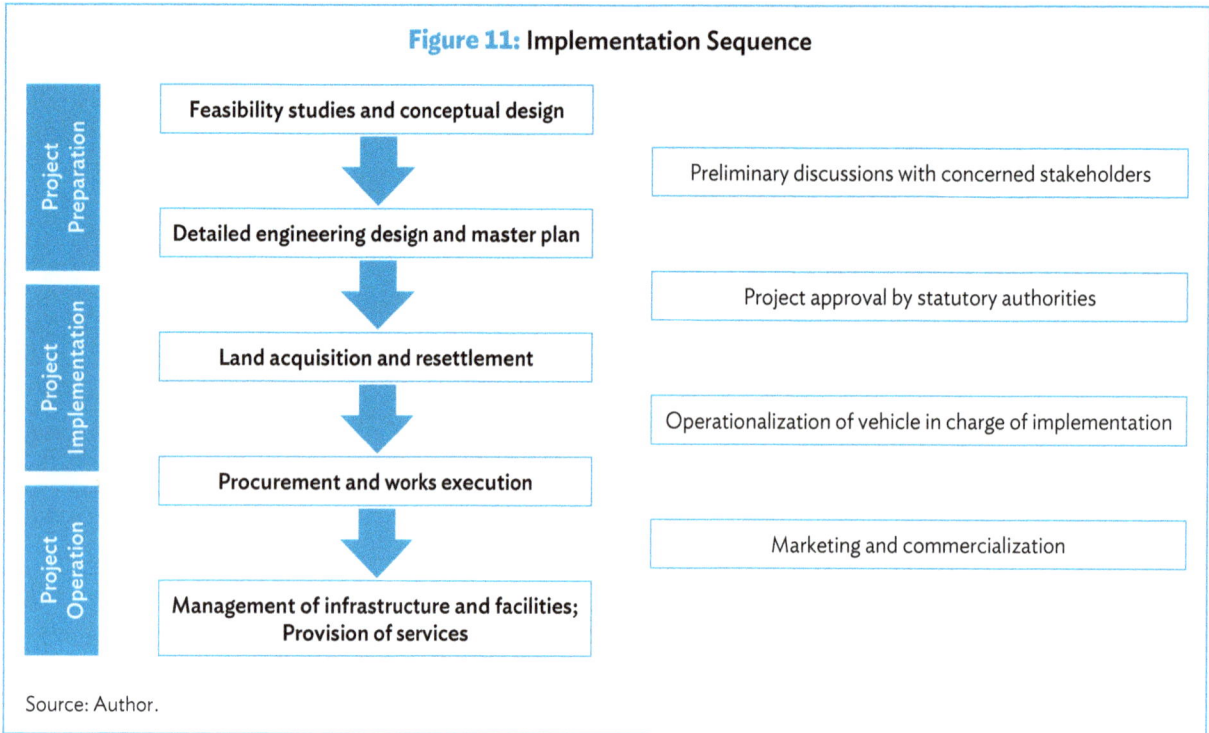

Figure 11: Implementation Sequence

Source: Author.

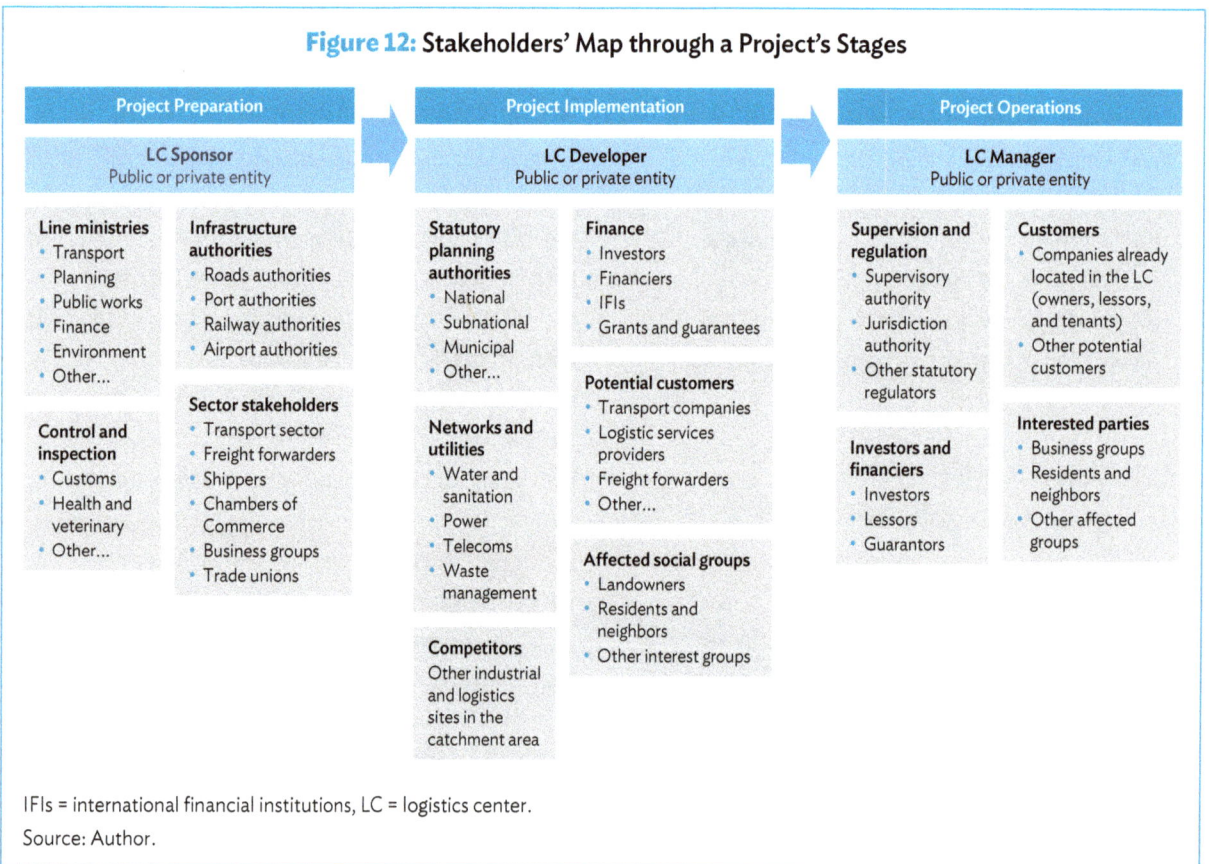

Figure 12: Stakeholders' Map through a Project's Stages

IFIs = international financial institutions, LC = logistics center.
Source: Author.

The value proposition of and access conditions to an LC need to be attractive to prospective customers and differentiated from the propositions made by competing developments in the same catchment area. Timing also matters: competing developers may move more quickly and attract demand for their premises before the LC project is fully implemented.

Once the LC is completed and plots of land and warehouses are sold or leased, the LC enters its operational phase. The entity operating the LC may be overseen by a supervisory or regulatory body. The entity itself may include a variety of shareholders and partners monitoring their investment and needing to honor their financial commitments. An LC should be managed so that shared-use infrastructure and facilities are up to the promised standards. Finally, some external interested parties may try to exert influence, e.g., business groups lobbying for reduced fares for the use of infrastructure, and residents or environmental groups lobbying for mitigation measures of some impacts.

4.1.3 What should be assessed during the project preparation stage?

The project preparation stage is key for the successful implementation of LC projects. Feasibility studies and conceptual design should assess the following issues:

- **Product definition and market alignment:**
  - ☐ Identification of target customers, related to their functions in transport and supply chains, e.g., transport companies, logistics operators, freight forwarders, and shippers.
  - ☐ Identification of customers related to their type of business, e.g., end users, investors, and auxiliary service providers.
  - ☐ Size of the market, current and forecasted.
  - ☐ Identification of strengths and project value proposition.
  - ☐ Identification of existing or planned competing projects.

- ☐ Definition of acceptable price ranges to potential customers.
- ☐ Identification of the preferred type of contracts by potential customers (acquisition of land, lease, rent).
- ☐ Identification of incentives, services, and specific legal conditions required or advisable to attract investment.

- **Location, land availability, and ownership:**
  - ☐ Evaluation of various location options.
  - ☐ Land availability.
  - ☐ Identification of any required resettlement of residents and businesses.
  - ☐ Anticipated costs for land acquisition and resettlement.
  - ☐ Assessment of legal property rights.
  - ☐ Proposal of land acquisition mechanisms.
  - ☐ In case of public domain land, specific legal and jurisdictional aspects.

- **Infrastructure issues:**
  - ☐ Identification of geologic, seismic, flooding, archeological sites, and other relevant risks and constraints.
  - ☐ Accessibility by road and other modes of transport where appropriate.
  - ☐ Availability of power, telecoms, and water supply, and connection to grids and networks.
  - ☐ Drainage and sanitation.
  - ☐ Impacts on existing infrastructure, e.g., pipelines, power lines, and roads.
  - ☐ Compliance with specific regulations and standards for infrastructure, e.g., roads, pipelines, and other networks.

- **Master plan blueprint:**
  - ☐ Functional design to optimize investment and operational costs.
  - ☐ Initial layout of plots to accommodate different types of market demands.
  - ☐ Measures to comply with land planning, infrastructure, and environmental regulations.
  - ☐ Definition of on-site and off-site required infrastructure.

- **Economic and financial study:**
  - ☐ Anticipated capital expenditure and operating costs.
  - ☐ Anticipated revenue flows and their segmentation (revenue from sales, leases, rents, and other formulas).
  - ☐ Necessary conditions to ensure financial feasibility.
  - ☐ Identification of financing needs and proposal of suitable capital/debt ratios.
  - ☐ Evaluation of different business models.
  - ☐ Economic impact assessment including cost–benefit study.
- **Anticipated environmental and social impacts:**
  - ☐ Impacts on protected or sensitive environments.
  - ☐ Anticipated impacts in terms of waste, noise, pollution, etc.
  - ☐ Expected territorial impacts, e.g., increased mobility, housing demand, public transport, and demand for other services.
  - ☐ Social impacts, e.g., jobs, economic growth, skills shortages and training needs, and gender issues.
- **Legal and institutional study:**
  - ☐ Coherence with government strategies, policies, and planning.
  - ☐ Identification of relevant stakeholders and statutory authorities, and their roles in project approval and implementation.
  - ☐ Evaluation of the legal and regulatory framework, in particular with regards to foreign investment and public–private partnerships (PPPs).
  - ☐ Risk assessment for the implementation stage and mitigation proposals.
  - ☐ Institutional architecture for the supervision and implementation entities.
  - ☐ Blueprint for marketing and commercial strategy, including guidelines for sale, lease, and rent contracts.
  - ☐ Business model proposal, including mechanisms for private sector participation.
  - ☐ Proposed organization structure for the entity in charge of implementation.

- **Implementation road map:**
  - ☐ Proposal of additional studies required for implementation.
  - ☐ Draft terms of reference for additional studies, detailed engineering design, and master plan.
  - ☐ Schedule of studies and engineering documents, approval process, operationalization of implementation entity, procurement, and works.

4.1.4 What should an engineering design and master plan include?

Designs and master plans for industrial areas are subject to national, subnational, and municipal planning and zoning regulations. A challenge that developers may find is that these regulations were not formulated with LCs in mind, and that they impose constraints to accommodate their specificities. A minimum list of aspects that should be included in engineering designs and master plans are:

- Definition of earthworks.
- Detailed road design, alignments, and grades, both for internal roads and off-site connecting roads, with the same for rail or waterways as appropriate, including loading and off-loading areas, storage areas, and other associated infrastructure and facilities.
- Detailed zoning of buildable and non-buildable areas including assigned uses. Definition of plot characteristics including minimum façade and plot surface and width. Definition of procedures to split or combine plots.
- Detailed design of water supply, drainage, wastewater treatment, and other networks, including associated infrastructure and equipment. Definition of other facilities and services, e.g., telecoms, public lighting, perimeter fence, internal surveillance systems, fire extinguishing system, irrigation, urban furniture, and signage.

- Design of green and open areas, parking areas, yards, and spaces for other infrastructure.
- Building parameters according to local regulations, e.g., floor area coefficients, maximum height, volumetric parameters, minimum distance to edges, and minimum quality standards.
- Detailed budget.
- Specification of technical conditions and standards for the execution of different work units.

4.1.5 What technical capabilities may be required?

LCs can be considered a specific kind of transport infrastructure, though they share many characteristics with industrial real estate developments. This means that engineering capabilities and skills used for the planning and design of transport infrastructure such as ports, roads, or railways may not be sufficient. Stakeholders interested in developing an LC may need to engage expertise in the following fields:

a. **Feasibility and conceptual design.** It is highly encouraged that projects start from a sound assessment of market conditions, a conceptual design that correctly identifies existing and anticipated demands, and a feasibility study that confirms the suitability of location, concept, and business model. These studies may require combining engineering, market, and business expertise into the field of logistics.

b. **Engineering design and urban planning**. This is for the elaboration and approval procedures of the LC master plan. Key experts should be familiar with the specificities of LC layouts as described in Section 3.2.

c. **Access infrastructure engineering.** Good access is key to an efficient LC and sometimes requires specific engineering capabilities be it for road access, rail, waterways, and also airport engineering in the case of air cargo centers.

d. **Warehouse design.** Increasingly becoming a specific niche, this is key not only for build-to-fit projects, i.e., warehouses designed to accommodate a specific company or process, but also for built-at-risk projects i.e., warehouses flexible enough to accommodate a range of potential tenants.

e. **Real estate commercial capabilities.** These are required when sponsors of LCs are infrastructure managers or government agencies with limited understanding of the real estate business.

f. **Environment and community engagement capabilities.** These are required when the project involves significant environmental and social impact on neighboring areas.

In some CAREC countries, some of these capabilities may be in short supply, especially in fields (a), (b), and (d). When this happens, local teams should cooperate with experts from places where logistics infrastructure is more developed.

4.1.6 What are the challenges of implementing a logistics center in developing countries?

Some general challenges may be found in developing countries where LCs are still a novelty:

- **Awareness.** Though many governments set goals to improve their country's logistics performance, awareness of the importance of land planning and logistics facilities to achieve those goals (i.e., the fourth pillar in Figure 1) is less widespread.
- **Transversal approach.** Logistics is governed by a variety of ministries and organizations that often have competing views and objectives. The development of LCs requires the alignment of a variety of actors with powers in transport infrastructure, land planning, customs, ports, and railways.

- **Capabilities and skills.** As explained in Section 4.2, LCs are different from ports and other transport infrastructure, and may require capacities and skills not common in typical transport and planning government agencies.
- **Concept and planning.** A follow-on from the previous is the flawed conceptualization and planning of LCs, often involving inappropriate locations, mismatch between demand forecasts and actual market size, unappealing conditions for potential customers, and other pitfalls. Some are discussed in Section 4.4.
- **Context enabler of win–win public–private cooperation.** A collaborative culture is conductive to the success of LCs, though often public and private sector stakeholders involved in logistics ignore or are suspicious of each other. Public sector stakeholders may lack a proper understanding of the private sector landscape including functions, priorities, operational practices, and the competitive environment of different players. On the other hand, big business may exert a disproportionate influence over institutions and officials ill-equipped to challenge them.
- **Implementation shortcomings**. Good schemes and master plans may be diluted by funding, procurement, and implementation shortcomings, e.g., insufficient resources are released so qualities and standards are reduced, contractors lack the capabilities to execute something different from usual business, or project management and monitoring is weak.

4.2 The Developer's Business Model

4.2.1 Who is the developer of a logistics center and what features should the developer have?

The developer is the entity in charge of the implementation of the LC and may eventually become the manager of the built complex.

It is important to understand the nature and functions of logistics services providers and those of LC developers and managers. Figure 13 illustrates some common models.

Model 1. One provider of logistics services builds and operates its own LC in exclusivity. Other companies not competing with the logistics provider but providing complementary services may also be located in the complex, e.g., fuel stations, banks, restaurants, and truck repair workshops.

Model 2. One provider of logistics services builds and operates its own LC, and uses most of its warehousing space. At the same time, it leases some remaining warehouse space to other companies such as logistics providers, manufacturers, distributors, wholesalers, and retailers. Other services, e.g., fuel stations, banks, restaurants, truck repair workshops, and foreign trade services, might also be located here.

Figure 13: Models of Logistics Services Providers' Involvement in Development of Logistics Centers

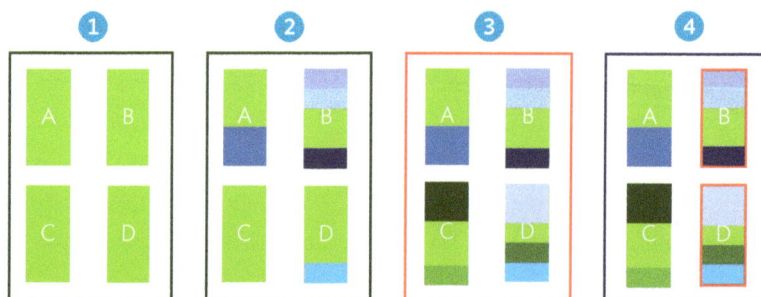

Source: Author.

In this case, the owner/manager of the LC is involved in two different businesses: provision of logistics services and real estate management. Sometimes, these two businesses may be carried out by different subsidiary companies within a single holding. Most LCs in CAREC countries, notably Kazakhstan and Uzbekistan, correspond to this model.

A drawback of this model is that logistics providers may not always be happy to use the facilities of a competing company, nor is it granted that the owner/manager of the LC offers equal opportunities to any interested company. Those least benefiting may be small- and medium-sized logistics companies lacking the financial muscle to build their own facilities and unwilling to locate in the facilities of a big player (or perhaps may be unwelcome there).

Model 3. A neutral party not involved in the logistics business builds and operates an LC, and sells or rents warehouse space to logistics services providers, transport companies, manufacturers, distributors, wholesalers, and retailers. Other services, e.g., fuel stations, banks, restaurants, truck repair workshops, and foreign trade services, can be located here as well. This model overcomes the concerns mentioned in Model 2. This neutral party developer will operate in the industrial real estate business, not in logistics, and its activity becomes closer to the development and management of a condominium than to the management of transport infrastructure such as ports or airports. Hence, its business performance is measured in terms of sold, rented, or leased square meters, rather than traffic throughput or tonnage as will happen with ports, airports, and railways. This is the most common model in developed countries.

The nature and partners of this neutral entity developing an LC is discussed in Section 4.2.2.

Model 4. This is a variation of models 2 and 3. In this case, the owner/manager of the LC sells or leases some plots of land (e.g., B and D in Figure 13) to a neutral real estate developer that builds and

maintains warehouses to be rented to logistics services providers or other customers. This is becoming very common in mature markets as logistics services providers prefer not to keep real estate assets and enjoy flexibility as their contracts with customers are increasingly short-term. This trend is leading to the emergence of many companies specialized in operating logistics real estate assets, many of them linked to pension or investment funds with a long-term vision.

4.2.2 What are the developer's options for public and private participation?

The developer can be a private sector entity, as is common in the development of industrial parks, a public sector entity, or a PPP. Public sector involvement up to some level in the entity in charge of LC development is common around the world for two main reasons: (i) to achieve the policy objectives as described in Section 2.2.3; and (ii) because the combination of higher costs and lower revenue (Section 3.2.4) makes LCs riskier and less attractive to conventional real estate developers.

PPP literature stipulates that both public and private partners should take the risks they are more capable of managing. Figure 14 illustrates risks along the preparation and implementation stages.

Though each project has its own characteristics, risks related to project approvals and land acquisition tend to be those that the private sector is less capable of managing.

This guide does not advocate for any specific model of public and private participation, though some features and recommendations for various possible situations are suggested in Table 3.

Figure 14: Risks Along the Implementation Sequence

	Risks
Feasibility studies and conceptual design	Insufficient, inaccurate information
Detailed engineering design and master plan	Delays in the approvals by statutory authorities / Requested changes distorting the initial concept and feasibility
Land acquisition and resettlement	Higher land and resettlement costs / Delays and litigation
Procurement and works execution	Construction delays and overruns / Poor delivery from contractor
	Demand less than anticipated / Market pushing prices downward
Management of infrastructure and facilities; Provision of services	Poor management affecting maintenance and service standards

Project Preparation; Project Implementation; Project Operation

Source: Author.

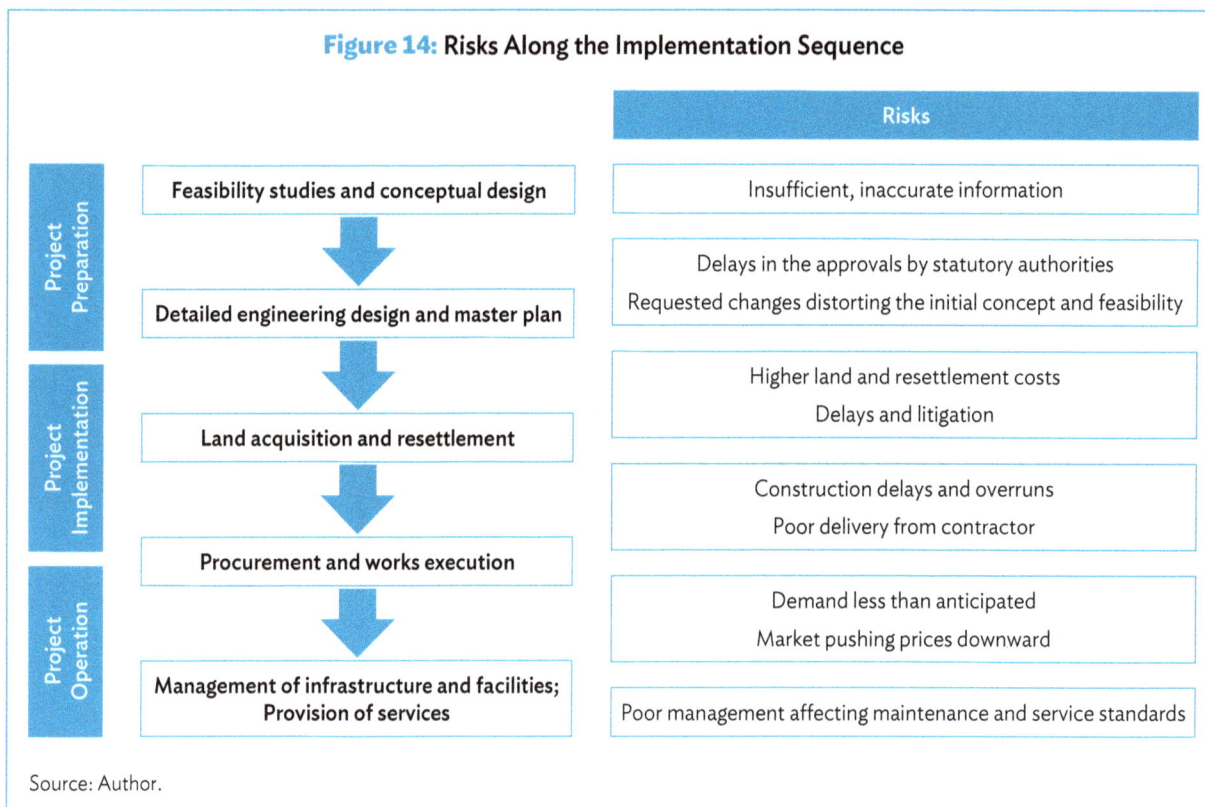

Table 3: Features and Recommendations for Various Public–Private Sector Combinations

A. Full public sector

Features	Recommendations
• The developer is a 100% public sector entity.	• A corporatized undertaking is better than an administrative body.
• Public sector assumes all risks, including commercial risks that it is ill-prepared to manage.	• Create a flexible and professionalized organization.
• Aspires to maximize economic and social benefits and alignment with transport and logistics policies.	• Establish sound governance and oversight frameworks, including independent persons on governing boards.
• Risk of bureaucratization, administrative rigidities, political interference, and affected by changes in the political context.	• Avoid capture by specific and/or private interests.

B. Joint venture

Features	Recommendations
• The developer is a company involving public and private sector shareholders.	• Identify the most appropriate type of partner (investor, specialized operator, builder, others). Avoid conflict of interests.
• Risks are shared between public and private shareholders.	• Sometimes private partners enter or expand their participation when the project has already progressed through early stages involving more risks.
• If private sector participation is low, the company may still be subject to public sector procurement regulations and rigidities.	• Public sector keeps some control over strategic decisions while day-to-day management is entrusted to the private side to improve efficiency.
• Need to manage eventual conflicting priorities between private and public partners.	

continued on next page

Table 3: continued

C. Public–private partnerships

Features	Recommendations
• The typical structure is public sector retaining land ownership and granting a long-term lease or concession to a private company charged with development, commercialization, and management. This is a very common arrangement for intermodal LC developed on land owned by ports, airports, or railway authorities. • The developer performance is monitored by the landlord to comply with contractual conditions. • Sale of land is not permitted, and lease/rent prices may be regulated, thus limiting the commercial options offered by the developer to potential customers. • Some upfront investment (e.g., earthworks and basic infrastructure) may be made by the public sector landlord.	• PPP contracts should be long enough to allow sufficient time for payback and acceptable profitability and, at the same time, be flexible enough to adapt to changing environmental conditions. • An attractive value proposition and the possibility of long-term contracts must be offered to potential customers to compensate for the impossibility of buying property. Value proposition is more obvious in intermodal centers adjacent to ports, airports, or railway terminals, but less so for road-only LCs, where these types of arrangements may be less attractive to customers. • Include mechanisms so that maintenance and upkeep is not neglected by the lessor during the last years of the contract period.

D. Segmentation per area or business unit

Features	Recommendations
• This model happens when the LC is created from portions of land with different natures (e.g., an LC created from railways land that cannot legally be sold and private land acquired in the market), or when the LC includes functional areas for different purposes (e.g., an LC including a marketable area dedicated to warehouses and a truck park that is managed as a not-for-profit operation). • Sometimes the public sector retains some pieces of land earmarked for strategic projects or public service activities within an LC.	• An integrated management or coordination body to ensure coherence and synergies among the different areas. • Set mechanisms to avoid public and private actors competing for the same type of customers.

E. Full private sector

Features	Recommendations
• The private sector manages the whole project cycle and takes all risks. • High efficiency and reactivity to market demands. • Private sector developments may benefit from some public sector support, e.g., off-site investments, streamline planning and approval procedures, tax incentives, and special legal regime.	• Land planning regulations should ensure that developments happen in suitable locations and reduce negative impacts. • A level playing field should be granted to avoid unfair competition when public sector support is provided to some developers.

LC = logistics center, PPP = public–private partnership.
Source: Author.

4.2.3 Sell, lease, or rent?

The options offered to companies interested in locating in an LC is of paramount importance for the commercial success of the developer and for its financial sustainability.

In some LCs, sales may not be an option as the complex has been developed on public domain land that cannot be legally sold. In some jurisdictions, land that has been acquired by a government entity may also have some constraints on sales to private parties.

In other circumstances, the developer may have a variety of options for transferring land rights to customers:

- selling or leasing portions of non-developed land that a second-tier developer will develop and commercialize;
- leasing portions of developed land, typically to second-tier developers that will build and rent warehouses for a set period;
- selling plots of developed land to end-users or to developers that will build warehouses for rent or sale; and
- building warehouses to be offered in the rental market. This option can take either of two forms: (i) build-at-risk i.e., start building without any formal commitment by an interested tenant and (ii) build-to-suit i.e., building is triggered by a commitment to rent for a minimum period from one or various tenants that have a voice in the design and standards of the new building to accommodate their specific operational needs.

Selling plots or keeping ownership to build warehouses to be rented are the two most common choices. The aspects that developers should consider when assessing these choices are illustrated in Table 4.

From the point of view of demand, some potential customers may feel more reassured buying property, perceived as a more stable, long-term investment. Others, in particular small companies, may not have the resources to buy, nor the willingness to engage in building their premises.

The trend in most developed countries is that logistics operators opt for renting warehouses as a more flexible solution, allowing them to focus on their core business. This has led to the emergence of a variety of companies specialized in the development and management of warehouses, usually associated with investment funds focused on a long-term horizon.

In this context, the recommendations to the developer of an LC are to

- engage in market research to identify the needs and expectations of your potential customers;
- whenever possible offer a product mix including plots for sale and warehouse space for sale and for rent; and
- adapt your product mix to your financial structure to avoid becoming too leveraged.

Table 4: Pros and Cons of Sale and Rent

Sale	Rental
Fewer fixed assets on balance sheets require less capital and financing.	More fixed assets on balance sheets requires more capital and finance.
Shorter payback period.	Longer payback period.
Commercialization activities are concentrated during one period, and end when all plots are sold.	Commercialization activities are continuous as contracts terminate or are renegotiated, and tenants come and go.
Little long-term recurring revenue.	Long-term stream of recurring revenue.
Business horizon is short term, so more exposed to economic cycles.	Business horizon is long term, so less exposed economic cycles.
The developer has little capacity to address inappropriate behavior by companies once property has been sold.	The developer as landlord has levers to address inappropriate behavior by tenants.
Less exposure to risks associated with asset depreciation.	Need to allocate resources to fund depreciation and repairs on assets.
Lower value addition entails lower long-term profitability.	Higher value addition entails higher long-term profitability.

Source: Author.

Public sector developers may be willing to maintain ownership of some property in LCs so that some activities of public interest can be hosted, and they remain in a stronger position regarding the day-to-day management of the complex.

4.2.4 What other businesses can be located in a logistics center?

A variety of other businesses apart from warehouses can be located in LCs. These include business that can provide

- synergies with the activities of transport and logistics companies;
- amenities to staff and visitors to the LC;
- value-added services to companies operating in the LC;
- services to commercial vehicles and their drivers; and
- additional and diversified revenue streams to the LC developer/manager.

A list of some of these possible services is described in Table 5.

Some services may be provided commercially, while others on a not-for-profit basis as benefits to companies and staff.

4.2.5 Should other manufacturing and service activities be located in logistics centers?

LCs may host a wider range of activities such as manufacturing and services beyond their typical targets. Targeting a wider range of potential customers, i.e., beyond transport and logistics companies, is a commercial advantage for the developer and may help reach financial breakeven in projects located in less attractive locations for the logistics industry.

Some aspects to be considered when assessing the range of acceptable activities within LCs include:

- **Incompatibilities.** Activities attracting many vehicles and visitors (e.g., shopping malls), may interfere with the efficient and safe operations of trucks. Mention of shopping malls is made because they are activities also searching for well-connected locations near major cities. Some LC developments do include more profitable office and commercial spaces well beyond the needs of LC users so that the whole project becomes more profitable. Other incompatibilities may be related to industrial hazards.
- **Unnecessary investment.** The specific features of LCs may involve higher development costs than conventional industrial parks, as discussed in sections 3.2.2 and 3.2.4. Letting in other activities that may not need the standards provided by LC may become a waste of resources.

Table 5: Possible Services at Logistics Centers

Services to companies	Services to vehicles	Services to staff and visitors
• Offices hosting freight forwarders, insurance, foreign trade services	• Fuel stations	• Restaurants and cafeterias
• Customs and inspections services	• Truck parks	• Hotels
• Shared services center	• Vehicle repair workshops	• Convenience stores
• Bank branches including ATMs	• Vehicle inspection facilities	• Training facilities
• Bonded warehouses	• Driver rest areas	• Nurseries
• Shared cold rooms		• Prayer rooms
• Rental and repair of handling equipment		• Public transportation

Source: Author.

- **Deviation from original purpose.** Many LC projects receive some government support in a variety of forms that stem from logistics policies. If an LC hosts a range of companies substantially different from those targeted, the policies' objectives may not be achieved.
- **Misalignment of interests among companies.** Transport and logistics companies share similar needs and concerns. This helps reach consensus when discussing maintenance costs for shared infrastructure, standards of service (e.g., access control and surveillance), or pooling resources. Companies with different needs may jeopardize this consensus.

When considering projects including a wide range of activities, it is sensible to clearly separate the logistics precinct from other non-synergic activities, including independent access and parking areas.[25]

4.3 Operations and Management of Logistics Centers

4.3.1 Who is the logistics center manager?

As mentioned, the entity in charge of the development of an LC may also manage the complex once construction is completed and companies settle in. Alternatively, management functions may be assigned to another entity once the complex is completed.

The nature of this management entity highly depends on whether the developer has kept ownership rights so that companies are mostly lessors or tenants, or it has opted to sell property so that its functions dilute once plots are sold.

However, it is common that sales contracts set provisions so that buyers adhere to a management entity assigned with the provision of some basic services as well as with maintenance of shared-use infrastructure and upkeep of public spaces, similar to a condominium community or an owners' association.

4.3.2 What functions should the logistics center manager perform?

Though they depend on LC type, size, and complexity, desirable functions may include

- internal administration, e.g., management of fees payment and receipts for shared services and facilities (e.g., public lightning, maintenance and upkeep, road cleaning, and waste collection);
- set rules for good use and tidiness of shared spaces and facilities (e.g., internal roads, car and truck parks, internal roads, and rest areas) and monitor compliance;
- set maintenance standards for shared infrastructure and facilities and contract required services to providers;
- monitor controlled access and security services;
- monitor compliance of minimum standards in services delivered by third parties in the LC;
- promote synergies among companies located in the LC; and
- promote recycling and environmental good practice.

All these functions should be performed according to the needs and preferences of companies located at the LC. It is highly recommended that the manager creates an owners'/lessors' committee as a formal channel for dialogue and decision-making.

---

[25] Plaza project (Appendix 2) included a vast shopping mall with high visibility along the motorway that was separate from the logistics precinct. Damu (Box 4) includes an industrial area, a logistics area, and a rail terminal. Both the logistics and the rail terminal are closed precincts with controlled access, while the industrial area is not. Moreover, the business model is different: rent and lease at the logistics area, and sale at the industrial area.

The key priority of the LC manager should be the maintenance of infrastructure and shared use facilities. Too often roads and public infrastructure in industrial areas fall into neglect because municipal authorities do not prioritize repairing infrastructure in places with few residents (and voters), companies are not willing to invest outside their premises either, and there is no entity in charge of looking after the industrial park's infrastructure and coordinating all stakeholders. Roads and shared-use infrastructure is more critical in an LC than in conventional industrial parks. That is why the presence of an LC manager is paramount.

In addition, some LC managers adopt a highly proactive role, encouraging the structuration of a logistics cluster from the companies located in the LC, and engaging in national and international marketing and promotion campaigns. LC management entities may also adopt proactive activities promoting social inclusion, and good neighborhood or environmental policies. These activities may have a positive impact by promoting awareness and reputation not just of the LC itself but also its region and country.

Figure 15 illustrates the typical sources of revenue and expenditure in an LC management entity.

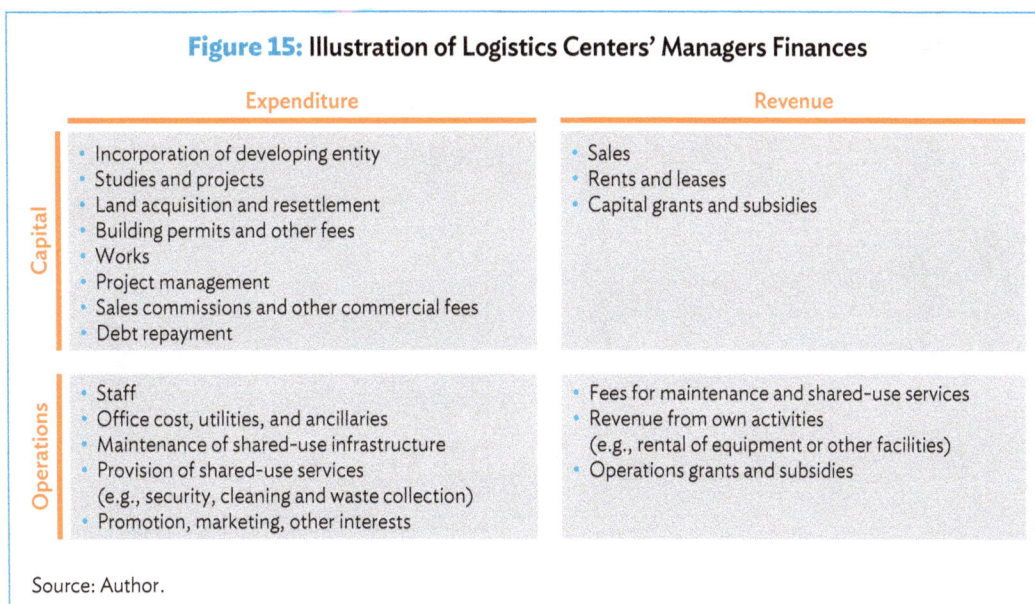

4.4 Typical Issues and Pitfalls

This section describes some typical issues and pitfalls found in the planning and implementation of LCs.

4.4.1 Insufficient understanding of the business of logistics centers by sponsors and planning authorities

The specificities of LCs are not always well understood by transport ministries, nor by port and transport infrastructure management authorities, where an engineering mindset is predominant. Successful planning and implementation of LCs require additional knowledge of urban planning, logistics operations, real estate, and commercial skills.

4.4.2 Logistics centers conceived as regional development tools

This is a very common pitfall. Some governments plan LCs under a supply-side logic in distant, underdeveloped, or thinly populated regions hoping that they may trigger economic development and jobs by attracting companies to these locations.

Figure 15: Illustration of Logistics Centers' Managers Finances

Expenditure	Revenue
Capital	
• Incorporation of developing entity • Studies and projects • Land acquisition and resettlement • Building permits and other fees • Works • Project management • Sales commissions and other commercial fees • Debt repayment	• Sales • Rents and leases • Capital grants and subsidies
Operations	
• Staff • Office cost, utilities, and ancillaries • Maintenance of shared-use infrastructure • Provision of shared-use services (e.g., security, cleaning and waste collection) • Promotion, marketing, other interests	• Fees for maintenance and shared-use services • Revenue from own activities (e.g., rental of equipment or other facilities) • Operations grants and subsidies

Source: Author.

However, location patterns of logistics companies usually work in the opposite direction: logistics are attracted to regions that are already major transport corridors or have a substantial manufacturing or consumer critical mass. Having said this, projects in less developed regions may be explored, adopting cautious phasing, adding flexibility to the concept, and including incentives. The example of Tunisia is explored in Box 5.

Box 5: Logistics Centers Strategy in Tunisia

Tunisia has a population of 11.8 million people, of whom approximately 2.5 million are concentrated in the Tunis metropolitan area, and where the country's main gateway, the port of Rades (container throughput 0.4 million twenty-foot equivalent units) is located.

Since 2011, successive governments have kept an interest in developing logistics centers (LCs) in various locations. Land adjacent to Rades port has been earmarked for off-dock logistics development for a long time, though it has not materialized because of geotechnic challenges. Other options have been explored. A feasibility study on a 200 hectare (ha) site located 25 kilometers (km) away from the city and 35 km from the port was funded by the European Investment Bank. The proposed site was found too distant and poorly connected, thus abandoned as a prospective LC.

More recently, the government has sponsored a 200 ha LC in Zarzis, a distant town in a little developed region near the border with Libya, with special economic zone status. And a greenfield deep-water port including an LC has been under discussion for years.

Most LC projects in Tunisia have been proposed with regional development in mind to create jobs in less developed districts, but have struggled to attract private partners to develop them.

Sources: Author; and Logistics in Tunisia.
http://www.transport.tn/fr/logistique/projet.

4.4.3 Project location driven by availability of land

The location of some LC projects may be decided based on availability of land (e.g., unused government-owned land, brownfield developments), irrespective of their attractiveness to logistics companies. Unsuitable or eccentric locations highly penalize the commercial success of LCs. Hence, location decisions should be based on a sound understanding of transport chains. Some examples illustrating this issue are described in Box 6.

4.4.4 Projects contaminated by vested interests

Vested interests may influence planning and commercial decisions to a point that the initial concept of an LC project can be diluted, and its purpose not achieved. Some examples of dangerous influences are

- location decision influenced by landowners' interests rather than by neutral assessment of operational and commercial aspects;
- project concept and location influenced by a single company, making the project less attractive to other competing companies; and
- industry organizations or lobbies influencing commercialization, setting barriers so that non-member companies are excluded.

4.4.5 Overoptimistic demand forecast

This is a typical flaw in transport infrastructure planning, as demand forecasts rarely account for slowdowns and economic cycles. LCs are more sensitive to inaccurate demand forecasts because they are managed as a business, thus the inability of a developer to achieve break-even in a reasonable period may lead to bankruptcy or a need for sponsors to bail out the development entity.

Box 6: Callao and Montevideo Logistics Center Projects

Callao

Callao Port is Peru's main gateway, handling 3.2 million twenty-foot equivalent units per year. The port's surroundings have been encroached by urban development so that containers from the terminals are shuttled by truck to off-dock terminals moving across densely populated areas and congested roads. These off-dock terminals have also become encroached themselves by residential and industrial areas. The only idle terrain in the area is in a military base owned by Peru's Navy. To improve logistics performance and reduce impacts, authorities envisaged the development of a logistics center (LC) to relocate off-dock terminals to this military terrain (approximately 33 hectares [ha]), an operation endorsed by the Navy.

Feasibility studies and a public–private partnership tender were prepared in 2013–2015. However no interested private sector parties could be found. This was due to (i) the perceived risks of the operation (proximity to military areas including ammunition depots, and some caveats requested by the Navy that would have limited the developer's leeway), (ii) high costs including the construction of a dedicated causeway above residential areas, and (iii) exploitation rights of a relatively small area during a too-short period of time.

Montevideo

The harbor in Montevideo, Uruguay's capital, is close to the old city and its only access is along the riverfront road. City authorities proposed developing an off-dock terminal and LC on 50 ha of municipally owned land located near the ring road. The site would be connected to the port by an 11-kilometer unused rail branch to shuttle containers in and out of the port. Port-related stakeholders were concerned by the additional costs, complexities, and delays caused by this rail shuttle. Other concerns were safety, because the rail branch had same-level crossings across the city, and noise, because rail movements were planned at night. The site is still earmarked for logistics activities by planning authorities though the rail connected off-dock terminal concept has been dropped in favor of supporting distribution platforms to service the metropolitan area.

The above examples illustrate that the mere existence of theoretically suitable locations do not guarantee the successful implementation of LCs if other functional and commercial aspects are insufficiently assessed.

Source: Author.

4.4.6 Stakeholders following their own agenda with conflicting interests

An LC developer may bring together sponsors with different and conflicting views on its concept and purpose. Port and railway authorities are often strong organizations and may view an LC project as a means to support their own agendas. Private stakeholders may be more focused on financial feasibility and less on policy views. A shared view about the LC concept and purpose needs to be achieved at the very early stages of project formulation.

4.4.7 Developer lacks right mandate and jurisdictional tools

This issue is most relevant for public sector developers. As discussed in this section, implementing an LC project requires a development entity. Sometimes this entity is created on purpose, sometimes another existing entity with another purpose and mandate is used. In any case there is a risk that the developer mandate and jurisdictional tools are not appropriate to successfully implement the project. Some of the shortfalls may be due to:

- Procurement rigidities to engage as a commercial undertaking to buy and sell assets.

- Incapacity to engage in transport infrastructure planning and implementation.
- Incapacity to engage directly or indirectly in forced land acquisition and resettlement.
- Incapacity to operate outside its statutory mandate (e.g., ports, airports).
- Incapacity or rigidities to engage in joint ventures or other public–private cooperation agreements.

An example of this situation is described in Box 7.

4.4.8 Developer becomes an overstaffed and cumbersome organization

This is also a risk that mostly affects public sector developers. Developers sometimes face a risk of becoming overstaffed due to a variety of reasons, including:

- Engineering and technical staff involved in planning and construction stages are kept onboard once the LC is built and much less technical work is needed.

Box 7: **Moroccan Agency for the Development of Logistics**

The Moroccan Agency for the Development of Logistics (AMDL) was created in 2011 to promote a national logistics strategy as well as regional logistics strategies, and has been championing logistics policies in the country covering infrastructure, training and skills, city logistics, and a logistics observatory.

Since its launch, the agency has actively promoted the concept of logistics centers (LCs) and even included a technical department for logistics zones within its organization. Despite this, the agency has been unable to engage directly in LC development projects because its mandate does not permit it. With no mandate nor capability to mobilize resources, AMDL struggles to align third partners, thus delaying implementation of the projects envisaged in the logistics strategies.

AMDL has nevertheless been successful in raising awareness about logistics in the country, as well as about the importance of improving technical and operational standards.

Zenata Logistics Center, in Greater Casablanca (Morocco). This LC was expected to be developed by three separate entities: the ports authority, the railways, and a public-sector transport and logistics company, with each owning substantial properties within the site, coordinated by AMDL. As of October 2022, the site has only been partially developed (photo by author).

- The development entity overstretches performing too many non-core functions without sufficient funding.
- Political interference in recruiting and in the scope of functions assigned to the development entity.

4.4.9 Insufficient abilities to negotiate win–win agreements

Officials in government bodies may have insufficient abilities to engage in constructive communication with the private sector. Similarly private sector stakeholders may have an insufficient understanding of public sector logic and constraints. Development and commercialization of an LC requires the alignment of public and private interests and the ability to speak the same language.

4.4.10 Long-term vision in planning but cautious short-term phasing

Policy makers may focus on the short term, while LCs are complex projects that may take time to implement. Short-term approaches may jeopardize meaningful projects. On the other extreme, implementing grand visions may lead to white elephants in the desert. Long-term vision is welcome. Wise policy makers and planners should reserve strategic pieces of land earmarked for logistics activities before other opportunistic activities are built on them.

At the same time, project development should progress cautiously to make sure that supply is aligned with demand and that the project remains adaptable to accommodate unforeseen needs.

4.4.11 Gold plating

As a rule of thumb, design of LC infrastructure, service buildings, and warehouses should be guided by operational efficiency and not by architectural glamor. Transport and logistics companies operate in highly competitive markets with low margins; thus they are not prepared to pay for overpriced real estate products. Products combining efficiency and architectural quality are possible, but the limits of trade-offs should be understood.

4.4.12 Logistics sprawl

Insufficient allocation of available land earmarked for transport and logistics in municipal or metropolitan land use master plans, or insufficient control of urban sprawl, leads to so-called logistics sprawl, meaning that logistics companies locate in ever more distant locations. Longer distances lead to increased transport costs, more congested roads, and more pollution.

It is recommended that available land for LC enlargement is maintained and that land for future residential and commercial developments is kept at some distance to avoid encroachments and other physical obstacles.

5

IMPACTS OF LOGISTICS CENTERS

5.1 Economic and Social Impacts

5.1.1 What is the economic impact of logistics centers?

Average costs of building LC infrastructure, e.g., earthworks, roads, access, drainage, sanitation, utilities networks, and warehouses, are highly dependent on the type of terrain, size, need of off-site connecting infrastructure, location-dependent unit costs, and quality standards.

Once built, warehouses may be equipped with storage racks, sorting devices, cold equipment, and other fixed assets. Forklifts and other handling equipment will be required as well as safety, fire extinguishing, and security systems. Offices will need to be equipped, including with IT systems.

As illustrated in Table 6, a developer investing $5 million in a 20 ha LC might induce private investment in warehouses and equipment amounting to $52 million–$58 million, i.e., $1 invested in LC infrastructure may trigger $10–$12 of investment in buildings and equipment by transport and logistics companies.

Table 6: Investment Ratios in Logistics Centers

Item	Cost Rate	Example for a 20-Hectare Logistics Center
Infrastructure	$250,000 per hectare (gross surface)	5
Class A warehouse	$400–$500 per square meter (m²) of covered surface	27–33
Fixed and mobile handling equipment	approx. $350 per m² of covered surface	23
Office equipment and information technology	approx. $35 per m² of covered surface	2.3

Notes: Infrastructure costs are variable depending on start conditions of the terrain. Unit costs may also vary greatly between countries. The proposed ratio comes from author's calculations and information from various projects in Kazakhstan. For Class A warehouses, cost estimates come from those received from stakeholders in Georgia, Kazakhstan, and Uzbekistan. Costs do not include cold rooms. As a rule of thumb, cold rooms may cost an additional $100 per cubic meter. For warehouses, it is assumed that only one third of gross surface is buildable area, with the rest being roads, open areas, parking, and maneuvering areas. Ratios for fixed and mobile equipment, offices, and information technology come author's experience in various projects in Western Europe, applying a 30% reduction. Costs for intermodal rail–road–waterways facilities are not included in the table.

Source: Author.

5.1.2 What is the jobs impact of opening a logistics center?

Functions in warehouses are diverse and so are their employment needs. As a rule of thumb, high turnaround activities will employ more people than low turnaround ones. High turnaround platforms employ around 10–15 people per 1,000 m^2 of warehouse space. A low turnaround warehouse's ratio may be 3–9 people per 1,000 m^2.[26]

Automation inside warehouses may reduce low-skilled jobs but increase high-skilled ones. The number of jobs will increase if value-addition activities apart from purely storage and handling are performed.

An LC also creates jobs in administration and services, especially if the LC has office space, and jobs for drivers who will not necessarily be employed by companies located in the LC. As a rule of thumb, about 30% of people working in an LC will perform management and administrative functions, 30% will perform operational functions, and 30% will perform transport functions, leaving 10% to other activities.

Groups opposing the construction of an LC in their neighborhood may argue that LCs provide lighter job density than other manufacturing and service activities. While this may be correct if seen from a narrow perspective, logistics functions are increasingly embedded within value chains in many manufacturing processes, so efficient logistics ensure the competitiveness of these manufacturing companies. Logistics is also essential to ensure deliveries to consumers. Distribution functions are also more anchored to the areas they are servicing than manufacturing and service activities, which face higher risks of being offshored. Job ratios at LCs may also increase if logistics operations include value-addition activities such as packaging, customization, labelling, and final assembly of components. Complementary activities located at service centers in LCs also contribute to heavier job density.

Examples of value-addition activities. Labor-intensive, value-adding activities including repackaging and customization being carried out at (left) DB Schenker at 10th of Ramadan Logistics Park, Egypt and (right) Familia Group at Medellin, Colombia (photos by author).

---

[26]   I. Ragas. 2012. *Centros Logísticos. Planificación, promoción y gestión de centros de actividades logísticas.* Barcelona: Marge Books (in Spanish).

5.2 Environmental Impacts and Mitigation Strategies

5.2.1 Air emissions

LCs attract a high number of heavy vehicles and most of them are likely to be powered by diesel engines. However, vehicles in LCs usually move only a short distance and are parked for loading and unloading, keeping engines off. Moreover, since little if any manufacturing is performed in LCs, emissions from machinery is very limited. Handling vehicles and equipment used inside warehouses are usually electric. Only forklifts or reach stackers for outdoor use may have internal combustion engines.

The impact of LCs on air emissions needs to be approached from a broad perspective. Though LCs may be considered as local source of emissions, notably particulate pollutants (nitrous oxide, and nitrogen dioxide from diesel engine exhausts), they can potentially contribute to an overall reduction of emissions if their location and operations reduce the number of heavy vehicles moving in and out of cities, along with the congestion associated with them. Effective LC locations may also optimize drayage routes and promote the use of vehicles with optimal payload capacity for first and last-mile routes.

5.2.2 Mobility

LCs' impacts on mobility need to be seen from two points of view. From one, the impact of heavy vehicles on congestion in the areas surrounding LCs can be mitigated with access roads and connections having sufficient capacity and avoiding bottlenecks. Access roads to LCs should avoid crossing residential areas. Truck and van mobility in LCs usually have a wave pattern, featuring a peak in early morning hours when vehicles start distribution rounds and a second peak in the afternoon when they return to base and long-distance haulage trucks leave for overnight routes.

From the other side is staff mobility. Their movement peaks coincide with those of trucks. Since LCs may be located at some distance from residential areas, car usage by staff may be high. Congestion and conflicts between trucks and cars can be mitigated by offering good public transport options.

5.2.3 Water and liquid waste

LCs' water consumption tends to be low and most is associated with human use, not any manufacturing process. Thus, liquid waste has few chemical or hazardous pollutants and can be treated in plants similar to those used for residential areas. Both rainwater and used water may be reused for refrigeration, sanitation, or watering gardens and green areas.

5.2.4 Solid waste

Solid waste at LCs tends to be largely associated with packaging, i.e., plastics, cardboard, and pallets. In the absence of manufacturing, offices and human activity are the other major sources of waste. Waste from packaging may attain significant volumes. LC managers may engage in pooling the contracting of waste collection and management. They may also facilitate circular economy schemes, i.e., some companies reusing materials that are waste for others. A typical case is the reuse of pallets.

Some companies operating at LCs may handle hazardous materials, e.g., chemicals and flammable liquids. These companies should manage their specific types of waste according to regulations and never compromise the safety of other companies nor the environment.

Vehicles and handling equipment may be a source of highly polluting waste such as batteries and used lubricants that need to be collected and managed safely.

5.2.5 Noise

Noise impacts tend to be lower than what would be expected because of the reasons described above: the absence of manufacturing processes and vehicles remaining parked most of the time. Noise may be higher along access roads, so noise screens may be appropriate if near residential areas.

5.2.6 Visual impact

Many factors may influence the visual impact of an LC such as size, height of warehouses, colors used on external walls, and the landscape where they are built. Environmental assessment studies should be made prior to the development of an LC and include an assessment of visual impacts and proposals for mitigation measures.

5.2.7 Safety

As discussed in Section 3.2.2, access and internal roads in LCs should be designed to ensure safe circulation and operations of heavy vehicles. When LCs have controlled access gates, safety and security is increased as the number of vehicles unrelated to the operations is reduced, making LCs safer environments for companies, staff, and drivers than other locations. Nevertheless, the fact that LCs concentrate large numbers of heavy vehicles means safety operations need to be a top priority. It is highly recommended that pedestrian corridors are clearly set with appropriate signages.

In addition, it is recommended that LC managers create safety and work hazard mitigation measures and guidelines for companies located and operating in the LCs. Some suggestions are to

- include a provision in leasing/rental contracts requiring complete compliance with local safety and work hazard regulations;
- ensure that work hazard and safety measures are also followed by visitors and third parties carrying out any activity in the LC;
- avoid the circulation of forklifts and handling vehicles outside warehouses, terminals, and storage yards; and
- set clearly marked emergency exits and meeting points in case of emergency and run drills periodically.

6

LOOKING AHEAD

6.1 What Industry Trends Will Shape Logistics Facilities Development?

- **Information technology.** The introduction of IT in logistics operations is unstoppable and will shape the characteristics of warehouses as IT requirements include enabling infrastructure. For instance, radio frequency identification tags and track and trace procedures are impossible to implement if cargo is still stacked on the ground; forklifts, stackers, and self-guiding devices cannot circulate on uneven floors or oddly shaped warehouses; and automated sorter devices make no sense in warehouses with few loading docks. More automation and IT will foster demand for higher standards in warehouses and logistics facilities. Moreover, LC developers need to pay as much attention to broadband connectivity as to road and rail access.

- **Logistics outsourcing.** Logistics providers will increasingly offer value-addition services. While first- and second-party logistics as shown in Figure 9 are low margin/highly competitive activities, third- and fourth-party logistics require more complex organizations and allow higher margins. More sophisticated logistics services will demand higher standards of infrastructure.

- **Value chain integration.** Logistics facilities should provide enabling conditions and spaces to accommodate ever more complex arrangements involving suppliers, customers, verification/certification entities, and so on.

- **Specialized logistics developers.** Specialized logistics developers, though common in more mature markets, are only starting to appear in CAREC countries.[27] Some private logistics services providers that developed their own LCs are moving into this business. Though still perceived as frontier markets, international developers may start investing in CAREC countries as demand for high-quality logistics space increases.

- **E-commerce.** The fast growth of e-commerce is disrupting conventional distribution channels and bringing innovation and new concepts into last-mile distribution. New facilities are being required to process this skyrocketing market, e.g., fulfillment centers at city level or micro-hubs at neighborhood level.

- **E-vehicles and alternative fuels.** Greenhouse gas reduction commitments are leading to the introduction of electric, hybrid, and hydrogen-powered vehicles. Since e-vehicles seem more adapted to last-mile distribution, local distribution platforms will require e-charging stations for their vehicles.[28] Some large warehouse projects are designed to include solar panels on their roofs

---

[27] Some well-known international companies of this type are Prologis (https://www.prologis.com/); Goodman (https://www.goodman.com/), and Panattoni (https://www.panattoni.com/). A wide number of smaller companies operate in this business at regional or national level.

[28] International Transport Forum. 2020. How Urban Delivery Vehicles Can Boost Electric Mobility. *International Transport Forum Policy Papers.* No. 81. Paris: OECD Publishing.

so as to produce green hydrogen to be used by resident trucks. These features will have an impact on how warehouses are designed in the future.

6.2 What Are the Boundary Conditions and Regulatory Trends?

- **Introduction of international standards.** The increasing integration of CAREC countries' supply chains at regional and global level brings a requirement to adopt international standards for quality, safety, reliability, and tracking and tracing. As for IT, it is harder to comply with these standards from legacy underperforming warehouses, thus increasing the demand for more modern facilities.

- **Carbon neutrality.** Governments are increasingly pushing for carbon neutral policies to comply with international emissions targets. These will require operational and transport patterns incompatible with legacy infrastructure and inefficient locations.

- **Legacy infrastructure lifetime.** Many small- and medium-sized transport and logistics companies have operated so far using legacy infrastructure built during Soviet times. These facilities are reaching the end of their lifeline. This is a challenge as the cost of redeveloping brownfield sites is high but also an opportunity to upgrade infrastructure.

- **Encroachment of existing facilities.** Some legacy logistics facilities and railway terminals are in inner-city locations and are already encroached upon by residential areas. Inner-city facilities are usually affected by shortage of space (e.g., short rail terminals, and insufficient stacking and storage areas), legacy layouts, complex internal operations, congested access, and impossibility of expansion. It is likely that companies may wish to operate from new and efficient facilities that will

likely be in suburban locations. More vocal city logistics and land-planning policies from municipal authorities are also likely to push some activities out of inner-city locations.

6.3 What Opportunities Exist for CAREC Countries?

- **Growth in transport and trade.** In most CAREC countries, logistics is already a booming industry underpinned by the development of trade corridors running both east–west and north–south, as well as by growing demand in domestic and regional markets. All this leads to an increasing need for LCs.

- **Ambitious infrastructure projects.** Opportunities for new LCs are also emerging from ambitious infrastructure projects such as ports along the Indian Ocean, Black Sea, and Caspian Sea, multimodal facilities along trade corridors, and from new rail and road links.[29]

- **Opportunities from rail-centered logistics.** The key role of railways is not only a source of legacy inefficiencies but also of opportunities. Railways are natural enablers of LCs as they require consolidation of cargo leading to the critical mass required for LC developments. Railway property also offer a wide range of opportunities for LC development within or close to main cities.

- **Land availability.** In some, though not all countries, land availability is not yet a major issue in many locations and land planning and its enforcement is more consolidated that in other developing countries.

- **Exposure to international practice.** Being at the crossroads of East Asia and Europe, CAREC countries are familiar with transport, industry, and operational standards of developed economies.

---

[29] It is worth highlighting the importance of the United Nations Economic Commission for Asia and Pacific Trans Asia Railway network, which provides alternative options to CAREC countries, including landlocked countries, to trade with Europe using efficient rail transport.

6.4 What Developments Should Be Avoided?

- **Artificial protection of internal markets.** Measures to protect internal markets may become barriers against innovative players thus delaying the adoption of international best practice, both in terms of infrastructure development and operational practice.
- **The region becoming a corridor.** The CAREC region is perceived as a land of logistics opportunity as new east–west and north–south trade and transport corridors are developed. However, little value addition and logistics services will happen if cargo only moves across CAREC countries, i.e., East Asia to Europe, or the Russian Federation to the Indian Ocean. Efforts should be made to integrate value addition and logistics services within the CAREC region. Some interesting approaches are being made for the economic corridors Almaty–Bishkek and Shymkent–Tashkent–Khujand.
- **Land-planning myopia.** As discussed in this guide, LCs require substantial areas of well-connected land. Other land users are also attracted by these locations. Land-planning schemes need to identify and reserve pieces of land in strategic locations near infrastructure, so logistics developments are possible in the short, medium, and long term.
- **Oligopolies.** If the development of LCs is monopolized by big players in the logistics market, the access of small- and medium-sized enterprises to modern logistics infrastructure may be jeopardized and thus their possibility of growing and creating a more competitive market will be curtailed.

6.5 What Are Suggested Next Steps for the CAREC Program?

CAREC brings together a range of key public and private stakeholders that are involved in transport, railways, and trade in the region. Taking advantage of its already well-established network of decision makers and professionals, the CAREC program could engage in further sharing of expertise, knowledge, and experience in the field of LCs. CAREC countries, in particular those where the concept of LCs is less developed, may benefit from exchanging experiences with other countries in the region and beyond. It may also help to set common warehouse standards and align them with those in other regions. Some suggested ideas are to:

- organize **regional workshops** on the issue involving international actors so broadening perspectives, and eventually holding study visits to best practice locations. These **workshops should reach decision makers at municipal and subnational level** involved in land planning and economic development, since experience in other countries shows that stakeholders at subnational level are key to enable successful LC developments.
- create a **database of projects** and best practices within the CAREC region. Presentations of best practice and site visits could be organized.
- create a **focus group** on LCs within CAREC, bringing together the most interested public and private sector stakeholders to discuss enabling conditions and barriers in the region. It would be interesting to engage some logistics associations already emerging in the region in this group. This focus group could analyze and recommend enabling factors with further detail than this guide has been able to present. The focus group could eventually evolve into a CAREC Association of Logistics Centers.

LOGISTICS CENTERS IN CAREC COUNTRIES

Azerbaijan

The Government of Azerbaijan approved the *Logistics and Trade Development Road Map for the Republic of Azerbaijan* and in 2019 the Ministry of Economy prepared various feasibility studies for regional trade and logistics centers (LCs).[1]

The **Red Bridge** customs border crossing, which includes a trade facilitation center covering 9 hectares (ha), is being implemented with United Nations Development Programme and European Union support. Similar trade facilitation facilities at **Khanoba** on the border with the Russian Federation have been completed, while the **Alat Free Economic Zone**, encompassing more than 600 ha, plans to attract internationally oriented logistics.[2]

Additional private sector initiatives include:

- **Absheron Logistics Center.** Located on the outskirts of Baku and covering 66 ha, this center resulted from the relocation of various inner-city facilities in 2018. It includes a rail terminal as well as storage, office rental, transport, and third-party logistics services.[3]

An aerial view of Absheron Logistics Center. It includes a rail terminal as well as storage, office rental, transport, and third-party logistics services (photo courtesy of Absheron Port).

---

[1]   Government of Azerbaijan. 2016. *Strategic Road Map for Development of Logistics and Trade in the Republic of Azerbaijan.* https://monitoring.az/assets/upload/files/4eae769862be45d63dcd5b50b1d31844.pdf.

[2]   Alat Free Economic Zone. https://afez.az.

[3]   Absheron Logistics Center. https://absheronport.az/en/page/haqqimizda/merkez-haqqinda.

- **Meyveli Bazaar.** Meyveli Bazaar, opened in 2008, is a wholesale food market that includes other ancillary services. Located beside the ring road of Baku, it offers good connections to the Absheron peninsula.
- **Food City.** Located near the border with the Russian Federation, this project aims to consolidate and facilitate exports of agricultural produce and will include auction and e-market services, as well as other ancillary services.[4]

Georgia

The main identified projects are:

- **Kumisi and Kutaisi LCs.** The Government of Georgia has been exploring the feasibility of LC projects in Kumisi (near Tbilisi, 43 ha) and Kutaisi (39 ha). As of June 2022, these projects were being reviewed.
- **Anaklia.** The government plans to provide 1,000 ha of land for the development of a new deep-sea port and free industrial zone that may include logistics.
- **Poti.** APM Terminals says it is engaged in a 100 ha expansion plan that will include a new multipurpose terminal that may also include some off-dock logistics facilities.
- **Private sector developments.** Though not proper LCs, a few modern warehouses have been developed near Tbilisi airport by international companies. Some companies are exploring the development of LCs near Tbilisi.[5]

Kazakhstan

The Government of Kazakhstan has regulated the concept of LCs and set some guidelines for infrastructure and services. According to the government, 22 transport and logistics centers (TLC) have been identified in Kazakhstan providing Class A warehouses as well as a range of transportation, customs clearance, and storage services. The largest ones are

- **Damu.** This private sector LC is located on the outskirts of Almaty. Opened in 2004, it pioneered the introduction of LCs in Kazakhstan.
- **Continental TLC Astana.** This joint venture between public and private partners is being implemented on the outskirts of Astana city providing state of the art facilities and various foreign trade services, e.g., customs, banks, regulatory authorities (phytosanitary, quarantine and transport control), customs brokers, certification bodies, insurance, etc. Current phase covering 30 ha was completed in 2015 with the possibility of expansion, and includes a rail terminal. It is focused on food distribution and has extensive cold facilities.
- **Continental Logistics Shymkent**, commissioned in 2018.
- **Special Economic Zone Khorgos–Eastern Gates.** Located at the border with the People's Republic of China.

Other operational private sector-led LCs are Astyk LC and Sapa LC, both in the Astana area, and ALG LC in Almaty. Other projects announced and at different stages of development are in Aktobe, Pavlodar, Almaty, Uralsk, Atyrau, Aktau, Kostanay, and Ust-Kamenogorsk.[6]

---

[4] Food City Agropark. https://www.foodcity.az/.

[5] Author's site visits; discussions with stakeholders and APM Terminals; and Invest in Georgia. https://investingeorgia.org/en.

[6] Author's site visits; discussions with stakeholders; ADB. 2021. *Ports and Logistics Scoping Study*. Manila; and United Nations Economic and Social Commission for Europe. 2019. *Logistics and Transport Competitiveness in Kazakhstan*.

Logistics centers in Kazakhstan. Continental LC in Astana (top) and ALG LC in Almaty (bottom) (photos by author).

Kyrgyz Republic

The Government of the Kyrgyz Republic has announced logistics centers in **Osh**, **Manas Airport**, **Balykchi**, and **Sary-Tash**, as well as the **At-Bashi Free Trade Logistics Complex**.[7]

Pakistan

Pakistan's National Freight and Logistics Policy prepared by the Ministry of Communications in 2020 includes proposals that are aligned with LC concepts such as

- integrating logistics considerations in special economic zones and industrial parks to facilitate efficient movement of goods;
- establishing cross-dock stations on cities' outskirts. These stations should be located near strategic, accessible locations to facilitate transfer, collection, and repacking of cargo;
- establishing urban consolidation/LCs in major cities; and
- encouraging multiple channels of private sector investment funds, particularly the application of the Real Estate Investment Trust to finance logistics infrastructure.[8]

The government's National Logistics Cell operates dry ports including in **Lahore**, **Quetta**, **Hyderabad**, and **Karachi**.[9] Private operators also operate some dry ports. Some dry ports include warehousing and storage facilities.

Tajikistan

The government announced projects including **LC Pyanji Poyon** at the border with Afghanistan and **LC in Sugd Region**, the feasibility of which is being assessed within the framework of the Shymkent–Tashkent–Khujand Economic Corridor.[10]

Uzbekistan

A Ministry of Transport database identifies around 200 private operational warehouses, of which 18 are considered Class A, offering storage capacity totaling 9 million tons. They include

- **Highway Logistics Center** (a road-only LC including a truck park, repair workshop, and cleaning and other services for vehicles and drivers), **Orient Logistics Center**, and **ULS** (both including a rail terminal and warehousing) in Tashkent. These are operated by the private sector conglomerate Orient Group, currently the national champion in LCs development, and also active in real estate, textile, and retail sectors.
- **United Cargo Centre**, also in Tashkent, offers road and rail connection and warehousing;
- **Termez Cargo**, a private center offering warehousing and office space at the border with Afghanistan;[11]

---

[7] *Kabar*. 2019. Largest Investment Park and Logistics Center to be Built in Osh. 15 April. http://en.kabar.kg/news/largest-investment-park-and-logistics-center-to-be-built-in-osh/; *Kabar*. 2020. Logistics Center – Locomotive for Development of Regions and Economy of Kyrgyzstan. 23 January. http://en.kabar.kg/news/logistics-center-locomotive-for-development-of-regions-and-economy-of-kyrgyzstan/; and background information to prepare ADB. 2021. *Ports and Logistics Scoping Study in CAREC Countries*. Manila. This included the review of all country presentations at CAREC Transport Sector Coordination Committees from 2014–2019 (both years included).

[8] Ministry of Communications. 2020. *National Freight and Logistics Policy*. Final draft.

[9] National Logistics Cell. Dry ports. https://www.nlc.com.pk/dry-ports/index.htm.

[10] Asian Development Bank (ADB). 2021. *Ports and Logistics Scoping Study in CAREC Countries*. Manila. https://www.adb.org/publications/ports-logistics-scoping-study-carec-countries; and discussions with ADB stakeholders. The information on Afghanistan was collected from international sources.

[11] The information on Afghanistan was collected from international sources.

- **LC Angren**, a 24 ha center developed by a joint venture between automobile and oil distribution companies and the government as a rail–road transshipment point (for mostly car industry cargo). It includes a variety of complementary services. The construction of a rail tunnel under Khamchik Davoni Pass has since made transshipment redundant, substantially reducing the center's activity and leaving it struggling to find new markets; and

- **Customs Border Terminal Yallama**, a customs inspection point that also provides storage capacity and services. A similar project is planned for Andijan.[12]

Logistics centers in Uzbekistan. Highway (top) and Orient (bottom) LCs (photos by author).

---

[12] Author's site visits and discussions with stakeholders. For more information on some of the mentioned projects, see Orient Group. https://orientgroup.uz/logistics; UCC. https://ucc.uz/; Termez Cargo. http://termezcargo.com/en/home; and Angren. https://clangren.uz/.

EXAMPLES OF LOGISTICS CENTERS IN EUROPE AND THE UNITED STATES

Rotterdam Distriparks, the Netherlands

Rotterdam is the biggest port in Europe in terms of traffic and a pioneer in the development of port-related logistics centers (LCs), named *distriparks* there. There are various *distriparks* along the more than 30-kilometer length of port facilities: Botlek, Eemhaven, Maasvlakte, and the Rotterdam Food Hub.

These port-centered LCs have multiple purposes:

- to attract and secure calls of shipping lines as more cargo is "tied" to the operations of logistics companies located in the *distripark*;
- to increase the economic potential of the port's business ecosystem as it includes value-adding logistics activities in addition to traditional maritime business; and
- to enhance the value of off-dock land assets and obtain an additional revenue stream from real estate business.[1]

Distriparks are located on port land and commercialized on leasing and rental contracts. Rotterdam port is owned by the city with a minority stake owned by the Dutch government.

Similar developments have been adopted in many ports across Europe and Asia. These developments require land, which is not always available in congested ports. In Rotterdam, Maasvlakte is located on reclaimed land, while in Barcelona a river mouth was displaced to make room for an LC.[2]

Freight Villages, Germany

Germany is a federal republic where states have significant powers, including strategic land planning, and resources. Most states have an active policy of reserving areas adjacent to rail–road–waterways' intermodal facilities and developing them for logistics activities, creating "freight villages", or GVZ in the German abbreviation. GVZs may be large, as in Nuremberg with 337 hectares (ha) or small. They are developed either by the state or in partnership with local authorities and private partners. The main logic underpinning GVZs has been multimodal transport facilitation by guaranteeing land with logistics facilities near intermodal transport nodes. Germany currently hosts more than 30 operational GVZs.[3]

---

[1] P. W. Langen. 2020. *Towards a Better Port Industry*. London: Routledge.

[2] For more information on port-related LCs see: Port of Rotterdam. Location options. https://www.portofrotterdam.com/en/setting/location-options; Port of Antwerp Bruges. https://www.portofantwerpbruges.com/en; Hamburger Hafen und Logistik AG. https://hhla.de/en; DP World. About London Gateway Logistics Park. https://www.dpworld.com/london-gateway/logistics-park/about-the-logistics-park; Marseille Fos; ZAL Port. https://zalport.com/en/home/; and Singapore.

[3] For more, see DGC. What is a Freight Village? https://www.gvz-org.de/en/freight-villages/.

Nuremberg freight village. Nuremberg freight village illustrates its trimodal nature, featuring a motorway connection (on the left), rail terminal (in the center), and inland waterways port (on the right). It also houses logistics functions such as containers and solid bulk near the riverport, containers, liquid bulk, and fuels near the rail terminal, and consolidation and transshipment platforms (photo courtesy of Bayernhafen Nuernberg).

Interporti, Italy

Italy has made a similar approach to Germany, creating intermodal logistics centers named *interporti*. More than 20 *interporti* have been developed and are managed under a variety of arrangements, including private partners and regional and local authorities as well as chambers of commerce and other industry groupings.[4]

Sogaris, France

Sogaris is a corporate entity created by the Paris city council and some other municipal councils and departments in its metropolitan area.

Sogaris' initial purpose was to develop a new wholesale food market in Rungis, in the suburbs of Paris, to replace old Les Halles facilities in the downtown, a project that included some warehousing space. After completion of Rungis market and LC in 1967, Rungis used its know-how to develop smaller-scale projects in other French cities. Recently, Sogaris has been very active in exploring innovative real estate solutions for city logistics challenges.[5]

Other regions in France have been active in developing LCs. Some interesting examples are Delta 3, Eurocentre, and CLESUD.[6]

[4]   Union Interporti Riuniti. https://www.unioneinterportiriuniti.org/.

[5]   Sogaris. https://www.sogaris.fr/.

[6]   Delta 3. http://www.delta-3.com/; Eurocentre. https://www.eurocentre.fr/index-fr.html; and CLESUD. http://www.clesud.fr/.

CIMALSA and Plaza, Spain

CIMALSA

Before the Olympic Games in 1992, most transport companies in Barcelona were in old facilities in a centrally located but degraded industrial area that acted as a barrier to the seaside. The city government planned an urban renewal scheme that included the Olympics Village and an initiative synchronized with the regional government to develop a new dedicated park (CIM Valles) to accommodate relocated transport companies.

CIM Valles was designed to include then state-of-the-art facilities to stimulate a much-needed modernization of transport companies. The entity charged with the development of CIM Valles (CIMALSA) is a commercial company 100% owned by the Government of Catalonia. After completion of CIM Valles, CIMALSA developed and managed similar projects in other regional cities as well as rail-to-road intermodal facilities and truck parks.[7]

View of CIM Valles. CIM Valles was designed to include then state-of-the-art facilities to stimulate modernization of transport companies (photo courtesy of CIMALSA).

---

[7]   CIMALSA. https://cimalsa.cat/.

Plaza

Covering around 1,200 ha, Plaza in Zaragoza city is the largest logistics center in Europe in one single site. Its size is disproportionate to the city's population of around 750,000 and its economic weight. The project resulted from a regional government strategy eyeing an opportunity from utilizing four major assets: (i) location at the crossroads of Spain's major population and manufacturing regions, all within a distance that allows truck drivers to make a roundtrip in a working day, (ii) vast availability of flatland at very affordable prices, (iii) good road and rail connections plus an underused airport, and (iv) close proximity to a medium-sized city with a university that ensures a supply of a skilled labor force.

The project was launched in the early 2000s and implemented by a joint venture between the region and a local bank. It started with an aggressive commercial strategy to secure some anchor customers, one of them a leading global fashion retailer.

In 2 decades, Plaza has put Zaragoza on the map of global logistics hubs, and its airport has become the busiest air cargo node in Spain.

Regional stakeholders have invested in measures to increase national and international awareness and promote training, skills, and research in logistics.

Plaza's story has become an inspiration for other second-level cities and regions. However, the success of Plaza is not easily replicated because it is based on fundamental attributes that make the site attractive to customers for operational and economic reasons, and on a smart master plan that allowed flexibility to accommodate a wide range of customers.[8]

Plaza, Zaragoza. The logistics center with main road access can be seen at the front, the rail terminal on the left, and the airport at the back (photo courtesy of Aragon Logistica).

---

[8] Plaza Logistica. https://www.Plazalogistica.com/?lang=en; and ZLC. https://www.zlc.edu.es/.

United States

LCs in the United States are developed by the private sector for the most part, though some benefit from public sector incentives to attract companies, as well as from government investment in off-site or access infrastructure.

Interesting developments involve vast integrated rail-enabled logistics (while noting that railways are private in the United States). Two examples of rail-connected LCs are **Alliance Texas** and **Centerpoint Intermodal Center** (CIC) in Illinois. Alliance Texas' master plan covers around 11,000 ha that integrate an industrial airport and railway terminal with logistics, industrial, commercial, and even residential areas. CIC covers some 1,500 ha and includes a major railway terminal. The investment cost of CIC was $1.26 billion.

Both projects have benefited from some government support. At CIC, for example, the Illinois state government established the Joliet Arsenal Development Authority in 1995 to plan the development of the land now occupied by the LC. The authority produced a strategic plan for the development of this land and sold it to private developers. In Alliance Texas' case, the site was planned and implemented as a joint effort between the city of Fort Worth, the Federal Aviation Administration, and a private real estate developer.[9]

Alliance Texas. An example of a rail-connected LC (photo courtesy of Alliance Texas).

---

[9]   US Department of Transportation, Federal Highway Administration. Project Profile: CenterPoint Intermodal Center—Joliet; Alliance Texas; Centerpoint; and L. Blancas, G. Ollivier, and R. Bullock. 2015. Integrated Logistics Centers: Experience from North America and Options for China. *China Transport Topics*. No. 13. Washington, DC: World Bank.

www.ingramcontent.com/pod-product-compliance
Lightning Source LLC
Chambersburg PA
CBHW050051220326
41599CB00045B/7363